# The Consummate Communicator

## *Character Traits of True Professionals*

# The Consummate Communicator

## *Character Traits of True Professionals*

Amy S. Hamilton, PMP

ISBN-13: 978-0-9982746-7-6 (Hardcover)
ISBN-13: 978-0-9982746-5-2 (Softcover)
ISBN-13: 978-0-9982746-6-9 (E-book)

Edited by Jennifer Harshman, HarshmanServices.com
Cover Design and Interior Layout by James Woosley, FreeAgentPress.com

Published by Free Agent Press, FreeAgentPress.com
Satsuma, Alabama 36572
VID: 20200915

# *Dedication*

*Dedicated to Stephen Ewell,*
*a leader, a mentor, a friend.*

# CONTENTS

# Foreword

## *by James Stavridis*

---

**I AM TRULY HONORED TO** be a small part of the inspiration for this excellent business fable. This book is an interpretation that I very much endorse of what I have tried to build and bring together in the various teams I have worked with over the years. Amy provides a story that clearly describes the Character Traits of True Professionals that I have used in the past to create cultures of excellence.

When reading the early drafts of this document, I encouraged Amy to add an Innovation Cell. I have been an advocate for using Innovation Cells to harness the creativity and unique input from across an organization to make rapid improvements.

As part of the development for this book, Amy asked me several interview questions to include my advice on creating a clear mission and vision for an organization. Throughout this fable, she weaves into the story the importance of having a clear mission and vision. The main character ensures that the mission and vision are the first thing that the executive team addresses, and this is something I believe is critical to organizational success.

Another key issue addressed throughout the book is the concept of change and how difficult it can be to implement change in a large organization. When I was at the US Southern Command, I got rid of the traditional Napoleonic J-Code structure to align the organization with humanitarian affairs and disaster relief. In order to achieve this, I had to ensure that everyone was "in on the takeoff, so they can be in on the landing."

The development of my leadership philosophies and Character Traits of True Professionals has been established through my life experiences, beginning with my wonderful Mom and Dad. I have also had many wonderful mentors such as ADM Mike Mullen, the former Chairman of the Joint Chiefs of Staff. I also encourage reading books to continue to develop and exercise the mind. My books can be found using the links below.

**—James Stavridis, PhD**

Admiral, US Navy (Retired)

Supreme Allied Commander at NATO, 2009-2013

Dean, The Fletcher School of Law and Diplomacy (2013-2018)

Operating Executive, The Carlyle Group

1001 Pennsylvania Ave., NW

Washington, DC 20004

Chair of the Board of Counselors, McLarty Associates

781.333.1790

## Find me online:

- Website: www.admiralstav.com
- Facebook: James Stavridis
- Twitter: stavridisj

# CHARACTER TRAITS OF TRUE PROFESSIONALS

## CIVILITY

*Be kind, share credit, and maintain your sense of humor! Don't lose your temper.*

---

## QUIET CONFIDENCE

*Be calm and steady. Do not let your ego stand in the way of progress.*

---

## CREATIVITY

*Always ask how you can do things better.*

---

## TEAMWORK & COLLABORATION

*No one person is smarter than the entire organization working together.*

---

## HONESTY & INTEGRITY

*Never violate the law or regulations; tell the truth unflinchingly.*

# Characters

---

## Midtown Branch

Britney Johnson – Loan Officer
Mark Hughes – Branch Manager

## The Board

Travis Baum – Longtime friend of Jay
Brad Watts – Board Member
Howard Linton – Board Member
Derek Smith – Board Member
Alice Williams – Family founded the bank
Bart Williams – Family founded the bank
Bert Williams – Family founded the bank

## The C-Suite

Jay Admiral – CEO
Josh Williams – COO
Dylan Jones – CAO
Wendi Brown – CMO
Thomas Payne – CIO

## Under 30s Board

Heather Whitmere – Bank Branch
Park Wang – Accounting
Sean McDaniel – Operations
Jose Morales – Marketing
Ranjith Kumar – IT

## Jay's Staff

Martha – Admin from Regional Bank
Rob – Jay's admin from his old job
Dave – Innovation Cell
Dan – Innovation Cell

## IT Department

Nathan Riley – Lead in IT
Kevin Carpenter – Lead Cyber Security
Pam Henderson – IT Project Manager
Sandy Taylor – Cyber Security

# THE LINE

**JAY ADMIRAL LOOKED AT HIS** watch again while standing in the line to see a teller at the bank. He wondered how many of the six people were in line during their lunch hour. The woman in front of him continued to tap her shoe on the tiled floor, displaying her impatience.

"Next," cried out a teller who looked both frazzled and unhappy.

The woman who had been tapping her shoe moved to the teller window. Jay looked at his watch again. He had spent almost forty minutes at the bank so far and knew his request would take some time. He saw that some of the tellers had recently closed their windows and wondered why the bank didn't adjust staffing for those who could only come during their lunch hours. *Bankers' hours indeed*, he thought to himself.

"Next," the teller called out from the window next to the woman still tapping her shoe impatiently as her transaction was taking place. She was obviously annoyed and speaking slowly with a lowered voice and glaring at the woman sitting behind the bank counter.

Jay stepped up to the bank teller and smiled. "I would like to speak with someone about business loans, please."

The teller gave a tight smile. "I'll see if a loan manager is available."

She left her teller booth and walked to one of the offices. Jay stood quietly, overhearing the woman next to him argue with the teller about fees on her account. He also saw that several more people were in line, waiting for a bank teller, and these were the only two teller positions still open. Jay looked at his watch again. It was ten till one. He had been at the bank for 50 minutes and still not met with the loan manager.

The teller walked back with another woman, who was giving Jay an appraising stare. He could almost hear the calculations in her head as she observed his freshly purchased thrift store suit, worn shoes, and off-brand watch.

"Why don't we step over here to the side," she asked. "This way, Jenn can assist other customers."

Jay looked over his shoulder and saw the next man in line already starting to inch forward toward the bank teller. "Sure," Jay agreed and moved aside toward the end of the abandoned bank teller counters.

"I'm Britney," the loan officer said, not offering her hand to Jay.

"Jay Admiral," Jay said, holding out his hand. Britney shook it reluctantly. "I'd like to discuss some business loan options with you."

"I'm sorry," she said with a honey-sweet tone and a smile that didn't reach her eyes. "I am on my way out of the office. Why didn't you make an appointment online?"

"I tried to make an appointment online," Jay informed her, trying not to sound annoyed. "I haven't been able to successfully navigate your scheduling tool, so I came by during my lunch hour."

"I am afraid I have to be someplace this afternoon," she told Jay. "Let's schedule an appointment for half past noon, one day next week."

"What about tomorrow at noon," Jay asked. He also noted that she hadn't commented or been surprised that he hadn't been able to use the scheduling tool on the website.

She checked her smartphone and sighed. "Tuesday 12:45 next week is the soonest I can schedule you."

Jay could tell this was the best answer he would get. "Fine. I will be back on Tuesday at 12:45. Could I get your card with the appointment time in writing?" Jay asked politely.

"Certainly," Britney said, pulling out a business card and scribbling the date and time on the back. She handed it reluctantly to Jay.

"Thanks," Jay said, pocketing the card. "I am looking forward to seeing you next week."

"Have a great day," Britney said dismissively and turned away, heading back to her office.

Jay sighed as he walked out of the Regional Bank branch office.

# Home

**That evening at dinner, Jay** provided his wife with the details of his experience at the bank. "What do you think?" Jay concluded.

"Jay,"—Lauren smiled—"I think this will be a challenge, perhaps the biggest since you decided to leave the navy."

Jay Admiral had left a promising career in the US Navy to pursue other passions. "I know." Jay appreciated that his wife had stayed by his side through both the best and the worst times.

"Jay, you know I will support you no matter what decision you make."

Jay knew the truth of that statement. It had been a friend of Lauren's that helped him pick out his suit for his trip to the bank. Jay was constantly pursuing new ideas, and he was lucky to have a wife who was patient and understanding. The couple had two wonderful daughters who were both grown, and the oldest had recently been married.

"This won't be easy," Jay agreed. "I just feel that it is the right thing to do."

Lauren gave her husband a hug. "Looks like you need to get to bed early, then. Tomorrow will be a big day for you."

# The Board

---

**The next day, Jay Admiral** walked into the headquarters of Regional Bank wearing a Bass Brothers suit, Italian leather shoes, and a Swiss watch. He strode confidently into the conference room to meet with the board.

"Mister Admiral," Travis Baum said, extending his hand in greeting, "great to have you here." Travis was the chair of the board and had recommended him to the board.

"Let's get this meeting started," Travis said loudly, leading Jay to the table. The board was composed of seven members including Travis. They had all been informed of the ongoing negotiation process to hire Jay as the new CEO for Regional Bank. Despite some reservations from a few of the board members, Travis was positive of the outcome of the board meeting. The bank was floundering, and they needed Jay's experience, innovation, and creativity. He had a long history of turning struggling organizations around.

Travis went over Jay's background on why he had pursued him as a candidate for Regional Bank and why he felt the board should endorse his candidate. He included references to several articles about Jay in national business publications and top magazines. After providing the background and his endorsement for the candidate, he opened the floor to allow the board members to question Jay.

Brad Watts opened with a question that was on each of the board member's minds: "Jay, you have seen the numbers for Regional Bank, and it is clear that we are losing market share every quarter. What is your strategy to regain our market share?"

Jay smiled. "I have a history of dynamic leadership that has demonstrated my ability to create positive organizational change. I will use innovative methods to transition Regional Bank from a brick-and-mortar operation to a flexible financial institution that meets the needs of today's modern consumers." Jay had done his market research and knew the products of Regional

Bank weren't the problem; it was the service. This was ironic from an organization that prided itself on customer service. "In my proposal I have outlined several steps that I will take to improve customer service as well as streamline operations."

"Jay," Howard Linton began, "we have all read your credentials, which are impressive, but so were those of the last three CEOs we have let go. What makes you different?" This earned some murmuring from around the table. Over the past decade, under the control of three different very qualified CEOs, Regional Bank had continued its gradual and steady decline.

"Howard," Jay responded, "I have been studying your bank since Travis first approached me, and I wouldn't be here if I didn't think I could stop this decline and shift the numbers back into the black. I have three points I would like to make about why I am going to be successful.

"First," Jay said holding up one finger, "unlike your previous three CEOs, who were very senior, I have many years before retirement. This is not my swan song." The last three CEOs had been close to retirement, and each had left with their severance packages to sunny retirement resorts. Jay could see just the slightest of nods from a few of the board members.

"Second," Jay continued, "I am coming in with a more diverse background than only the financial sector." The previous three CEOs had come from within the financial sector. A few heads around the room nodded. Jay was a graduate from the United States Naval Academy in Annapolis, Maryland, and had served for five years, after which he had attended Yale Law School, where he studied business law. From there, he launched his career originally in acquisitions and mergers. Jay had quickly built a reputation as an astute negotiator, but more importantly had emerged as a consummate communicator. He had a rare gift of being able to communicate effectively with labor and management and across multiple industries. His success had led him to become the CEO of a large conglomerate he helped to acquire and then run. He loved taking on new challenges and demonstrating that leadership and professionalism were not bound by industry. Jay believed the key to success in any organization was being able to effectively communicate with the people in the organization, the customers outside of the organization, and the shareholders.

Not surprisingly, Alice Williams did not let Jay get to his third point and spoke next. She had made it clear from the beginning that she was skeptical of Travis's choice for CEO. "Mister Admiral," she cut in, "this bank was built on traditions and has a long and distinguished heritage. Your history demonstrates a need to shake things up and run unorthodox programs. What are your plans for Regional Bank?"

Jay had read the background information on each of the seven board members and had been prepared for Alice, the great granddaughter of the bank's founder, to oppose his appointment. "That's a great question, Alice." Jay focused directly on her and gave her an answer he knew she would not like. "I am going to bring Regional Bank to the modern age while respecting the traditions and values that made this bank successful in the past."

Alice scoffed. "We have online banking already. What will you do different?"

"Modern banks offer a convenient and comprehensive customer experience, more than simply having checking and savings online," Jay said patiently. "In addition, the in-house Internet Technology Department is an area where Regional Bank can save money and improve customer experience. Mobile banking, cloud technology, and social media are all areas where Regional Bank lags competitors. At the same time, Regional Bank's reputation of local community focus should be leveraged."

Alice challenged, "So, you are going to do exactly what our competitors do?"

Jay paused and looked around the room at each of the board members. "I can't predict at this point how I will 'shake things up' as Alice suggested. I went to one of the Regional Bank branches yesterday and experienced one of the worst customer service experiences at any bank ever. I had a long wait, and the staff avoided making eye contact with me." Jay looked around the room. "This from a bank that prides itself on customer service at its brick-and-mortar locations."

"Which branch?" Brad asked, clearly ready to hunt down the culprits.

"That's not relevant," Jay responded. "Who in this room uses other banks because Regional Bank does not offer the flexibility you need for today's modern business?"

Over half the heads in the room looked down. "Traitors," Alice said under her breath.

"Regional Bank needs to both modernize and get back to the basics at the same time," Jay told the room. "Right now, even the brick and mortar customer service is failing. Regional Bank needs to stop losing market share against its competitors. What I am offering Regional Bank is leadership, experience, professionalism, and most importantly, innovation."

"Speaking of innovation," Alice chimed in, "We have some concerns about the staff that you want to bring over to Regional Bank with you." Alice looked at Bert and Bart, who both nodded in agreement. "What exactly is this Innovation Cell you are requiring as part of your employment agreement?"

"Thanks, Alice,"—Jay smiled at her—"for bringing me back to my third point. I have been successful in the past due to encouraging creativity and innovation in organizations I lead."

"My Innovation Cell is a multidisciplinary team I have worked with in the past to create success," Jay told the board. "In summary, the cell is a basic unit of innovation, and when leveraged at the micro level can have macro effects across the organization. I have included examples of how successful innovation has occurred in organizations I have led in the past. To be honest, I don't know what they will find. I don't have all the answers, but we are stronger together and will find solutions as a team," Jay concluded.

"Does anyone have anything to add?" Travis looked around the quiet room. What Jay hadn't pointed out was that he really was their only option short of selling Regional Bank to a competitor at a rock-bottom price or dismantling it and selling it in pieces. Travis knew that Alice's cousins Bart and Bert would vote with Alice and that the other board member who had remained silent, Derek Smith, would most likely vote along with Howard.

"Let's take a vote." The room unanimously voted for Jay Admiral to be the next CEO of Regional Bank. He had one year to meet their numbers, or the bank would be sold.

"Congrats," Brad said to Jay, being the first to shake his hand.

Alice Williams still wasn't happy but knew Jay was the bank's best chance. "Good luck," she told Jay and honestly meant it.

Travis waited until the room was clear. "The board was the first step," he told Jay. "Now the rest is up to you."

Jay looked at his friend and smiled. "Guess this is a case of be careful about what you ask for. You just might get it."

"I was a little nervous that Alice and the other Williamses were going to balk at your requirement to have hiring and termination authority of the executives," Travis told him candidly. "The family is very protective."

Jay responded, "Travis, you know how I feel about my family, so I completely understand. As a matter of fact, I think I heard our wives planning a get-together soon."

# First Day

**Jay had researched the situation** at Regional Bank from the first day Travis had approached him. He knew the numbers showed declining market share and profit loss, but he felt that numbers were only one aspect of business. People are what made up an organization, and Jay needed to get to know the staff at Regional Bank before implementing change. He was bringing in a handful of members, to include his Innovation Cell and administrative support, from previous organizations. They would assist him in getting familiar with the organization quickly.

Rob had been Jay's assistant in his last position and was making the transition with him to Regional Bank. As Jay stepped into the office, he saw Rob and a silver-haired woman glaring at each other. "You must be Martha," Jay said smoothly, having been forewarned about the longtime executive secretary at Regional Bank. "I'm looking forward to working with you." Jay shook her hand smoothly. "I see you have met Rob."

"Yes," Martha said, "and I have informed him that I have been the executive secretary at Regional Bank for the past ten years."

"Great," Jay said. "Then you will have no problems showing Rob around, and between the two of you, I will know that I am in capable hands." He gave Rob a knowing look as he continued past the pair to the larger, inner office.

Jay spent the first few days attending briefings from the various departments. Each department had its own perspective on why the bank was struggling, and no department ever considered their own department at fault. Jay's innovation team leads, Dan and Dave, had been critical to his success in his last organization, and he knew he could count on them to find low-cost solutions, find the quick wins, and determine ways to address more complex problems within the organization. Jay knew he didn't have all the answers, but surrounding himself with members of his previous team who had helped him achieve success was a large part of how he knew he would achieve successful results at Regional Bank.

One of the greatest strengths of Regional Bank was that it was built on tradition, but this also created its greatest weakness. It was inflexible and unchanging. Alice was right. Jay would have to shake things up. He just needed some more information first, not the kind that could be obtained from a meeting room but from getting the opportunity to meet with people at various levels in the organization and understanding that the problems were multifaceted.

# Midtown with Britney

**When Tuesday lunchtime arrived, Jay** walked into the midtown Regional Branch Office. He had selected this office because it had the worst customer service ratings and didn't make quota on loans. Jay could see that the lines were even longer then when he had visited the branch the previous week.

"Mister Admiral," Britney said with a tight smile, approaching him swiftly, "I wasn't sure if you were going to be able to make this appointment."

"Why wouldn't I?" Jay responded.

"I expected a termination notice after reading that you were the new CEO of the company," she confessed.

Jay could tell Britney was upset and nervous about her current situation. "Let's go to your office and talk about last week," he urged her. Jay followed Britney to her office, where she looked around uncomfortably. "Sit at your desk," Jay motioned toward it. The office was rather small and impersonal with an office chair behind the desk and two uncomfortable-looking chairs for guests in front of the desk.

"Mister Admiral," Britney began, "I am sorry about last week, but you looked very different than you do now."

"I came in here last week to see how the average working-class person was treated by Regional Bank before accepting the position of CEO for this bank," Jay told her. "Based on my research and previous visits to other branches, the treatment I received was no surprise."

"Have you reviewed the bank's loan policies and standards, Mister Admiral," Britney asked, not knowing what to say to the new CEO.

"Tell me about them from your perspective," Jay responded, having reviewed them but wanting to know Britney's thoughts.

Britney had been venting her frustrations regarding the outdated and unachievable loan policies for the past two years. She only needed this minor encouragement from the new CEO to tell him her thoughts on the issue. "They are simply not achievable and allow for no flexibility on the part of the loan manager," she told him.

Jay nodded encouragingly.

"The quotas are so high that only the branches located in the very best locations, which means higher incomes than those in midtown, have a chance of achieving them. There is little opportunity for those in this neighborhood, so most clients go to the savings and loans, where they have a chance," Britney was very passionate in her delivery.

"I know that it makes us seem impersonal, but I didn't even make it close to the corporate quota when I used to listen to everyone's stories and needs. I had to quickly start taking only those that appeared they could obtain a loan with the strict corporate rules," Britney concluded, looking at Jay pleadingly for his understanding. "Even now, I am on probation because I haven't been able to make the unreasonable quotas set by headquarters."

Jay believed that most people came into work wanting to do a good job every day. That was one of his biggest reasons for meeting with Britney. He strongly suspected that there were significant gaps between management and practices at Regional Bank. When he had seen the reaction from members of the board about his visit to the branch, he knew he would have to handle things himself. This was a learning opportunity, not a witch hunt.

"Tell me what you would change," Jay instructed Britney.

After spending almost the entire 30 minutes Britney had scheduled for their discussion about Jay's "loan," he felt like he had enough information regarding the loan situation to go back to the office, but he still had another question before he left.

"Britney, I appreciate your honesty, and I want to discuss some more matters with you at a later date," he told her. "These are some difficult times for the bank, and we need to work as a true team, because it is using all of our resources that will get us through this. One thing I have observed here and at other branches is a lack of teller support during lunch hours. Let's discuss your thoughts on that the next time we meet."

"Thank you, Mister Admiral." Britney came around from behind the desk and shook hands with her CEO. "We only see the corporate management once a year unless they are coming for an inspection."

"Britney," Jay responded, "things are going to have to change for Regional Bank to stay in business. I need to hear the perspective from you and other members from various levels."

"I thought when you walked in, you were here to terminate me, Mister Admiral," Britney confessed.

"Instead, you listened to the problems we are having as loan officers. Even if you don't do anything else, that is more than any of your predecessors have done."

"It wouldn't be right to terminate someone for following policy," Jay told her. "Thanks for your time Britney. I'll be in touch. I also plan to send some of the members from my Innovation Cell to observe your operations. Either Rob or Martha from my office will contact you to coordinate." Jay wanted to get his innovation team leads, Dan and Dave, out among the staff to start looking for creative ways to solve Reginal Bank's problems.

When Jay stepped out of Britney's office, he immediately turned right into the branch manager's office. Mark Hughes looked up immediately and greeted the CEO. The walls were thin, and even though he hadn't been able to make out every word, he had been able to discern that Jay was saying his farewell to Britney. "Mister Admiral," Mark said, "is there anything I can do for you today?"

"Just wanted to let you know that I am going to send a few members from my innovation team over to do some observations," Jay told him. "Have a great day," Jay told the branch manager and walked out of the building, noting that the lines of 12:45 were gone and the bank had only a few customers at 1:15, but all the bank teller windows were fully staffed.

As soon as the CEO walked out the door, the branch manager and every teller who wasn't engaged with a customer swarmed over to Britney.

"He didn't say anything about firing you," the branch manager stated the obvious. "What did you discuss for half an hour? He didn't actually want a loan."

"He asked me about the loan policies and how I would change them," Britney told those assembled around her. "He even took notes regarding some of my suggestions and said he would be sending members of his team out here to observe more."

"Wow," one of the tellers said. "I think we are going to see some big changes with this new CEO."

"We have to," Britney responded. "If the numbers at Regional Bank don't improve, we will all be out of jobs. Even the fancy managers working uptown at headquarters."

"Let's get back to work and stop harassing poor Britney," the Branch Manager cut in, "even though I know you will each hound her individually for the details." He smiled and added, "I know I will."

# Administrative Strife

**When Jay arrived back at** his office, he could feel the tension between Martha and Rob. He was hoping the situation would work itself out.

"You have an executive meeting in five minutes, Mister Admiral," Martha informed him with a binder in her hands. "I have compiled all of the reports that the Chief Financial Officer, Chief Auditor, and Chief Marketing Officer have asked to discuss today."

Jay could see Rob sitting back at his desk. He had no doubt that Rob had advised Martha that the new

CEO wasn't going to go into his first executive meeting with business as usual.

"Thank you, Martha," Jay said, "but I think today will be my chance to establish things with my new team. I believe I mentioned that today we would review the Regional Bank vision, mission, and goals. In addition, I will share my leadership philosophy and character traits of true professionals with the team."

"Mister Admiral," Martha said, clearly unhappy with this decision, "Regional Bank is an old and established organization. We are not one of the mergers or start-ups you have dealt with in the past." Martha had worked her way to up to the role of executive secretary at Reginal Bank through decades of service. She had been the executive secretary for the previous five CEOs, to include the bank's heyday and more difficult recent times. She was viewed by those who had worked with her as both steady and professional. She felt it was one of her jobs to keep the executive office moving, even with the high turnover of CEOs.

Jay understood that change was difficult for his team members and remained calm. After all, *quiet confidence* was one of his character traits of true professionals, and he needed to display it in front of his new team. "I realize that you may think this isn't important, but in my experience, the first few months of an organization sets the tone. Business as usual hasn't been working for Regional Bank for quite some time. We are losing market share and profitability each quarter. The board hired me to create change, which may be hard for existing staff," he added, "but without change, Regional Bank will go out of business."

"I understand," Martha replied stiffly, clearly not on board with the change.

Jay knew it was important to help Martha adjust to change. "I appreciate that a lot of work goes into these reports," he told her. "There is so much work to do and not enough time to do it all in," Jay told Martha. "Since I am in meetings for the rest of the day, could you please summarize the reports and highlight what's important, pull any relevant background information, and add a paragraph or two on what you think is important for me to know?" Jay asked Martha.

Hesitantly, Martha said, "That has never been a part of my duties before." Martha had learned through her decades as an administrative assistant to keep her thoughts to herself and that the most important thing she could do for her bosses was to keep their affairs secret. When she had tried a few times to give her opinions about bank business, she had been promptly told to mind her own business.

"Martha," Jay smiled at her warmly, "I have no doubt that you have been reading these reports every week for years and have quite a few thoughts about their accuracy, history, and the current situation in each department. I would be a fool not to leverage your knowledge and experience in this organization."

Martha smiled slyly at Jay and Rob. "There have been a few occasions where I have felt that the reports don't quite reflect what I have heard from the admins down in the various departments, but none of the previous CEOs ever wanted to hear my opinion," she added a bit sourly.

"Things need to change," Jay told her again, this time knowing she was starting to see where she might fit into the future of Regional Bank. "I would like you to work with Rob on this. I want to get your expertise and experience combined with his fresh perspective."

"You would like me to make suggestions, Mister Admiral?" Martha responded with disbelief. She had given up making suggestions a long time ago in Regional Bank, and for the first time in many years, ideas that had been long buried were buzzing around in her head.

"I learned a long time ago that everyone on the team has something valuable to contribute," he reassured Martha. "I also think when we have unique partnership and pairings, we can see things differently than when we are all looking at things through the same lens."

"Please excuse me," Martha said and left the office. She felt out of breath, and for the first time in many years, her composure in the office was slipping. She had thought there wasn't anything a CEO could do to surprise her, but this one had just opened a door that she had thought was shut a long time ago.

"You handled that very well, boss," Rob told Jay. "I have been trying to get through to her for the past few days, and you achieved more in a few minutes with her than I did in all that time."

"It is going to be hard on some of the staff members who have been here a long time," Jay told Rob. "Martha needs help with the transition and is used doing things a certain way. She also needs to know she is relevant, and that change doesn't mean she will lose her job but that her job will be changing."

"To be honest, I am surprised Regional Bank is still in business if the administrative support is an example of the rest of the organization," Rob told his boss. "I feel like I stepped back in time in this office. Only the bare minimum has been automated."

"The good thing is that the processes are old and can easily be codified if they aren't already documented," Jay responded with optimism.

Rob laughed, "Good luck with the C-Suite. If they are like the rest of this place, you are in for a challenge."

"We," Jay emphasized. "We are in for a challenge."

# THE C-SUITE

**JAY HAD READ THE RESUMES,** bios, and online profiles, if they had them, of each of the members of the executive team and could recognize each on sight when he walked into his first executive team meeting. Describing the room as hostile would have been an understatement. New CEOs at Regional Bank had dismissed one or two of the previous executives and department heads very quickly in the past. Jay could tell each executive was prepared to defend their department as well as their own jobs.

Jay had deliberately waited until the clock changed to exactly the start time before entering the room. He didn't believe in keeping people waiting, but he did believe in being precisely on time and wanted to start with this new team setting a precedent. He also knew that today would set the tone for the months to follow, and this meeting was key to his getting the executives engaged.

"I know this is an old and established institution," Jay began, making eye contact with the members assembled around the table. "Today, instead of discussing the requested items, which are being reviewed, and I will have Martha or Rob send back to you with my notes, we will be discussing the mission and vision statements of Regional Bank. By the time we leave here today, I want each member of this executive team to understand what we are trying to accomplish in this organization and for each of you to be able to explain what this means to your direct reports." While Jay spoke, he passed around the folders that had been assembled with the proposed mission, vision, themes, and goals for the organization.

"This doesn't look very different from our current vision," Wendi Brown, the chief of Marketing commented, "but the minor changes add new energy to what has become tired and cliché."

"I think our current vision and mission are fine," Dylan Jones, the chief auditing officer said. "Why are we wasting time on this when we should be focused on compliance and other regulatory issues?" he grumbled.

Jay had expected some resistance but was glad it wasn't coming from Wendi. He needed Marketing and a few of the other executives to support him early. He knew from Wendi's bio that she had a strong background and had heard she was frustrated that she hadn't been able to push through some innovative marketing approaches. She was one of the newer members to the executive team.

"Our market share and profitability don't support your analysis, Dylan." Jay looked at several of the members, who appeared skeptical as well. "We won't create change by continuing to do what we have always done. That is the definition of insanity. I need this team to start looking at the strategic picture and start working as a wholistic team."

"We could use some more teamwork around here," Josh Williams, the Chief Operations Officer, said, looking specifically at Thomas Payne, the Chief Information Officer.

Before the Chief Information Officer could respond, Jay pointed out some cards located in their folders. "Those cards are drafts that contain the new vision, mission, themes, goals, and my character traits of true professionals. Once we agree on the details of the changes for the company items, these will go out to all employees. The character traits of true professionals are directly tied to my leadership philosophy, and I think it is important that every director in this room understand that I not only expect you to support these traits but to live by them." He looked around the room. "I also expect you to challenge me if you think there is a time when I am not living up to my own values about these traits."

The rest of the meeting was spent making small changes to Jay's proposed vision, mission, themes, and goals for Regional Bank. A few of the executives, like Wendi Brown, were excited to participate. A few like Dylan Jones were skeptical, and most were someplace in the middle. The one member who didn't participate was Thomas Payne, and this concerned Jay Admiral the most. At least when people openly dissented, they were part of the process. He had a feeling it was going to become an issue.

# #1: CIVILITY

*Be kind, share credit, and maintain your sense of humor! Don't lose your temper.*

---

WHEN JAY RETURNED TO HIS office, he wanted to capitalize on the progress he had made between Martha and Rob. Jay needed the new additions he brought to the office to be quickly accepted and integrated. Martha had been with Regional Bank for a long time, and her acceptance of the new members to the administrative team and the Innovation Cell would transfer to other long-established members.

"The executive meeting went as well as can be expected, and Wendi Brown from Marketing will be leading the initiative to get out the new vision, mission, themes, and goals to all the employees. In addition, I will be spearheading an effort to ensure everyone understands the Character Traits of True Professionals."

"How can we support?" Rob asked. Martha scowled at Rob. The new office dynamics were still uncomfortable for her, and she didn't like how eager the young man was to please the new boss. In her day, there were words to describe kids like Rob.

"The first trait I want everyone to focus on needs to be applied in this office. That trait is civility. My definition of *civility* is to be kind, share credit, maintain your sense of humor, and never lose your temper." He looked at both of his assistants. "For the past two days, this has not felt like a civil environment, and I need the two of you to work through this."

"Yes, Mister Admiral," Martha responded automatically from years of being tried to comply with whatever the CEO wanted. Of course, normally, that meant adjusting schedules or arranging travel.

"Of course," Rob responded, hoping the progress he had seen earlier would continue. The past hour working on summarizing the reports with Martha had actually been enjoyable.

"You each bring unique backgrounds and experiences with you to this position, and you need to be the examples to the rest of the organization on how we can combine the best of what has worked for Regional Bank with new and state-of-the-art processes and ways of thinking." Jay focused on Martha. "You have worked here for over forty years and bring a wealth of experience to this office. I am counting on you to tell me if I am repeating a mistake from the past."

"Mister Admiral," Martha responded, "it isn't my place to criticize you or tell you how to run the bank. I am the executive secretary." Martha had seen more administrative assistants fired for speaking up than she could count. She had made it to the executive secretary for the CEO at Regional Bank through extreme organization and time-management skills. Martha had recently read *Life is a Project* and begun to apply this mantra to every aspect of her job at Regional Bank.

"I appreciate your skills, and I can tell you keep things organized here," Jay told her. "Now I am asking you to expand your role by sharing with Rob and me when you think I am going too far off course or when you think I am making a mistake."

Rob decided to take the opportunity and added, "I know you think I am young and don't belong here, but what Mister Admiral is hoping for is that we can be a team. He is really big into teamwork, and this office needs your expertise and experience."

"How do I know you aren't just going to try to gain my knowledge from me and then terminate me?" Martha asked boldly. She was shocked after the words left her mouth. She was in unchartered waters.

Jay noted that this was yet another time someone at Regional Bank was concerned about their position of employment. He made a note to review the turnover rates and the reasons for terminations. If everyone was too focused on simply maintaining their jobs, it was no wonder the staff wasn't making suggestions about how to make improvements. He only had a year to turn this organization around, and at the moment, he was struggling to simply get his own assistants on the right track.

"You're right, Martha," Jay told her. "I might simply be trying to get the information I can out of you and then terminate you. I think you have a lot to offer and are an under-utilized resource here, though. You have seen plenty of executives go through this building and CEOs sit in this office. I would like your insights, but I know trust takes time." He looked to Rob and back to Martha. "I'm asking you to give us a chance to make some changes here to try to save Regional Bank."

Martha had seen the declining numbers over the past few years but never commented. It hadn't been her place. This was the first time any of the executives at Regional Bank had asked for her opinions on how the business ran and even though the past hour working on the summaries with Rob had been exciting, she still had reservations. "I will give it a try, Mister Admiral," Martha told the new CEO, "but it might take me some time."

"That's all I'm asking," Jay told her while handing her one of the prototype cards from the board meeting.

"I already see you as processing most of the traits of true professionals. I just think the three of us will have to work together for a while to really make them shine in you."

"Thank you, Mister Admiral," Martha replied, still a little leery of this new way of working together.

"Great," Jay responded. "I would like to do a no-notice walkthrough of each of the functional areas within the headquarters during the next week. Can the two of you work together on this? It is important that it doesn't show up on my calendar or anyone else's calendar."

Talking the hint from his boss that it was time for the two of them to leave the office, Rob decided to show Martha he could be a team player and admit his weaknesses in front of the boss.

"Can you show me the calendar system again?" Rob asked Martha. Rob recognized that he had to improve his relationship with Martha and hoped he was up to the task because Martha was the only one who understood how most of the antiquated IT systems worked. Why Regional Bank hadn't migrated to a modern system was baffling.

"One more thing," Jay added as they walked out the door. "Please have Josh Williams, the COO, meet with me as soon as possible. I would like to have a better understanding of Operations."

Martha smiled in response. "Yes, Mister Admiral." She was in her element scheduling meetings. She had scheduled some blind meetings for previous CEOs before, and she was looking forward to teaching Rob. Maybe they would be able to work alongside each other after all.

Jay reflected on his meeting with the executive team, and he had a lot of concerns. The team overall seemed very set in their ways, and the team had little diversity. Most of the members were older than him, and they were very focused on their stovepipes within the organization. The Chief Operations Officer, Josh Williams, appeared to understand the situation, and Jay needed to get together with him soon.

# Chief Operations Officer

"**THANKS FOR COMING BY ON** such short notice," Jay told Josh, getting up and shaking his hand. "Please have a seat."

Josh Williams had been the scapegoat for the past two CEOs who had passed through, but his love for the organization kept him inspired and willing to keep pushing. Three members of his family were on the board, with his aunt Alice being the most vocal. She aspired for him to be the CEO one day. The Williams family had been cornerstones of Regional Bank since it was founded, but Josh knew if the bank didn't turn around soon, there wouldn't be a bank. Unlike his aunt, who did not like Jay's coming to shake things up, Josh thought he might be just what the company needed.

"When the new CEO wants a meeting, very few things could be more important," Josh said truthfully.

"I wanted to observe you in the executive meeting before we spoke," Jay informed him candidly. "I would like to hear from you what you think of the current situation."

"I realize I am one of the youngest members of your executive team and many think that it is only my family that has gotten me to where I am, but I have worked hard and understand many of the internal issues in this organization," Josh took a breath and decided that blatant honesty was the only way to approach Jay Admiral. "I had conflict with the last two CEOs. They didn't want to take my advice and then blamed me when they failed. I don't expect the CEO to listen to everything I have to say, but I expect them to take responsibility when their decisions and poor choices result in increasing loss of market share and downward spirals in revenue."

"That's fair," Jay told him, "and I appreciate your frankness. Now that you have seen the changes I want to make to the vision, mission, themes, and goals of the organization, what are your thoughts?"

"I like that you stayed true to the core values of Regional Bank but are modernizing things to meet the advances in the world. I would like to be a part of the details. In the past, the CEOs kept things status quo, and as we continue to lose profitability and market share, we need to recognize that current operations aren't working," Josh added with some passion. This bank had been a part of his family for years, and he wanted to balance being true to the core principles while still staying in business. He also felt that in some cases, tradition had become dogma rather than being true to the original beliefs, such as ensuring entrepreneurs could get affordable loans for their businesses.

"To turn this ship around, I need to know that the key members are willing to follow my directions." Jay had been concerned that Josh might have the same bias as his aunt, but the younger Williams appeared to have a better grasp of the situation. "I admit I had some reservations before meeting you, but I am optimistic that we will be able to work together."

"I certainly think we will be able to work together," Josh agreed. "I have a lot of ideas, but many of them were not taken seriously by previous CEOs," Josh told the new CEO, gaining some enthusiasm. "We have some great people in this organization, but we have been doing the same things for so long that we aren't keeping up with our competitors."

"I had a meeting with one of the loan officers at the midtown branch at lunch today," Jay told him.

"Britney," Josh said quickly. "She is actually the only loan officer at that branch. Her boss Mark Hughes called me right after you left the office," Josh confided.

"Nice to hear that your branch manager is keeping you informed," Jay responded, pleased that Josh knew the details and the names of the key people at the branch. "She gave me some ideas on how she thought the loan process could be improved to serve her branch. What are your thoughts?" Jay asked, handing Josh a list of notes from the meeting.

"These are some great ideas," Josh told him. "Our mission statement talks about the financial well-being of all of our customers, but our loan policies don't support that. We used to be a bank that was more focused on our local customer base, but even some of the large commercial banks are providing better options to our region—and the credit unions are beating us hands down."

"Those are my initial thoughts," Jay responded. "I would like you to work on some ideas on how to improve the loan policies at this branch and any others that you think need it."

"I have some ideas already, and I think the branch managers and loan officers are going to be excited for the first time in a long time," Josh responded with conviction.

"My Innovation Cell leads are available and will also be looking at these and other concepts. Have you had a chance to meet with Dan and Dave yet?" Jay asked Josh.

"Yes," Josh responded. "I spoke with Dan earlier about the role of the Innovation Cell and how they can assist each of the departments as well as the entire organization to find ideas that can help us to accomplish our goals. I have read about concepts like innovation cells in some of the more forward-thinking business magazines, but this is the first time we have had anything like this here at Regional Bank."

"In addition, I have some concerns about the shifts for the tellers at the branches," Jay offered. "I also know that in the rest of the banking industry, they are called customer service representatives or CSRs, and we may want to think about how to modernize."

"Tradition is hard to die here at Regional Bank," Josh responded. "I will look into your concerns on both these matters."

"Great," Jay said. "Anything else?"

"One more question," Josh began. "I have never seen anything like your Character Traits of True Professionals before. Is that from when you were in the Navy?"

Jay smiled. "The Navy was a passion for me, and like all good sailors, I still feel the call of the sea, but life had other plans for me. One of the things the Navy taught me was what it takes to be a leader, and I try to bring those traits with me every day and apply them in everything I do."

"I appreciate it," Josh told him sincerely. "It is nice to know where the CEO stands."

"You brought up a good point at the beginning of our conversation about leaders being accountable. As my Chief Operations Officer, I expect you to let me know when I am not doing what I am saying," Jay said sincerely. "That's how I've always operated on any of my teams."

"Thanks for meeting with me, Mister Admiral," Josh said. "I will start on these policy issues at the branches and come back to you with recommendations."

"Jay," Jay responded.

"What?" Josh replied.

"Please call me Jay," he told Josh. He felt like he had just established a solid foundation with his COO and that Josh was in a critical position to help get Regional Bank growing again.

# Work Center Visits

**Jay was on his third** functional team visit the next day and was taking note of both positives and negatives he saw in each area. So far none of his chief executives appeared happy to see the new CEO show up at their work center. He had just walked into the work center for Wendi Brown, and she appeared the least annoyed. Wendi and her team were gathered around a smart board and were frantically brainstorming ideas just as the CEO entered. Jay brought Innovation team leads Dan and Dave with him and introduced them to each of the functional areas, trying to explain what the Innovation Cell would do and ensuring that functional leads were familiar with them and would be responsive to their requests in the future.

# The Marketing Department

"Mister Admiral," his Chief Marketing Officer addressed him when she realized why her team had gone silent. "We weren't expecting you. My staff is working very hard on your internal marketing project of sharing the new vision with the staff."

Jay felt that this was the first time that one of his executives had been concerned about Jay disrupting progress rather than the fact that Jay had not announced his visit in advance. "I don't want to interrupt the team at work," Jay told her, "but I am interested in seeing how progress is coming. Please continue."

"The question we were debating was how to ensure the branch offices get the same message," Wendi said to her team.

"We can send internal memos," one woman suggested.

"We can send out weekly e-mails," another team member suggested.

"We need to do more than just send e-mails," a young man said. "E-mail is for old people."

"José," Wendi responded, "Did you read the CEO's thoughts about teamwork? Even if you disagree with other suggestions, you need to be respectful to your teammates."

"Sorry," José said to the group in general, "but we need to start sharing information like start-ups or how we do things at home. We are missing out on a lot of opportunities."

"No worries," someone responded. "Every day I come into work, I feel like I stepped back in time a decade."

The group continued to dialogue and forgot that the CEO was listening to their brainstorming session. One thing that had become apparent from his visits to the other functional areas was that the IT Department was not meeting the requirements of their internal customers nor their external customers.

# The IT Department

**Walking into the basement of** the Regional Bank building, Jay Admiral took in the drab environment. The rest of the work centers had been correct that the IT Department was like stepping back in time and not in a nostalgic-photo way, but in a dead-dinosaurs way. When Jay stepped into the office, nobody looked up from their desks.

He approached the administrative assistant outside of Thomas Payne's office and smiled, "Hello, Meg. I am here to walk around the IT work center." He was glad that he had the forethought to have Martha provide him with the administrative assistant names for each department he was visiting.

"I'm sorry, sir," Meg said nervously, "I don't have you on the schedule, and Mister Payne does not like to be disturbed."

Jay could hear the steady clacking of keys all around him and no other sounds. He wondered briefly if Thomas Payne had a staff of humans or drones. "I realize that this isn't on the schedule. That is why these are surprise walk-arounds," Jay told Meg kindly. "No need to disturb Thomas. I will just introduce myself and my Innovation Cell leads around to the staff."

Meg sat frozen in place. At first, she had not recognized the new CEO, but realizing who he was, she still wasn't sure what to do. Mr. Payne was very rigid and had strict rules of not being disturbed. Mr. Admiral had seemed kind and was chatting quietly with one of the server administrators already. Meg decided the best way to handle the situation was to send Mr. Payne an e-mail about the situation. *This should address the situation*, Meg thought as she hit Send.

Thomas blinked twice as he read the e-mail from his administrative assistant. The subject line read, "Mr. Admiral is walking around the IT Department!" This administrative assistant had been with him for a while and generally understood his needs and requirements. She had never sent him such a strange message before. He responded to her e-mail with "I need more information. When is he coming?" Thomas Payne was a man who expected his staff to provide him all the details the first time, and he did not appreciate having to ask for details that should have been provided in the first place.

Meg decided to risk Mr. Payne's biting sarcastic comments and went into his office after getting his response. She stood barely in the doorway and said quietly, "Mister Admiral is talking to Nathan and some of the server administrators right now. He said you didn't need to be disturbed, but I thought you would want to know," Meg concluded, wringing her hands. She had no idea how Mr. Payne was going to react to this information. He was known for his sarcastic tongue and verbally embarrassing his staff in front of others.

"I'll see what this is about, since obviously my staff is too incompetent to track when the CEO is coming to visit my IT Department," Thomas glowered at his assistant and walked out the door.

As he stepped into the bay, he realized two things immediately. First, several of his staff members were sitting and standing around the CEO, and most were smiling. Second, the quiet clacking of keyboards was almost silenced as those employees still at their desks were straining to listen to the conversation.

"Nathan and I have had several discussions about how we could balance operations with cybersecurity," Kevin Carpenter told the new CEO.

Spotting Thomas standing outside his office, Jay hailed him over. "I was just getting to know your team, a room full of bright sharp minds. It looks like this bank has a lot of investment that needs to take place in the IT area."

"I have been requesting additional funds for my IT Department for years now," Thomas admitted, "but the previous executives turned us down in favor of other projects."

Jay could see the staff shift and look around nervously as the CIO entered the area. He decided to continue to address the team. "Tell me more about your ideas on mobile applications," he encouraged one of the team members.

Thomas responded before any of the members of his team could answer, "We don't have the expertise or in-house knowledge. I told the previous CEOs this before. Mobile applications and new technologies should be outsourced. I'm just happy if this group can manage to keep the e-mail servers up for a full day without something crashing," he added snarkily.

"It doesn't matter if the work is done in-house or outsourced," Jay responded diplomatically. "Our IT team can still contribute to the ideas and way forward. Based on cost–benefit analysis, we can decide which projects to add and the best way to get them accomplished." Jay could see that the IT Department members were looking uncomfortable and decided it was time to end the session. "I'd really like to thank the members of the IT team for sharing your thoughts with me. It looks like there are a lot of opportunities down here. My innovation leads are available for you to run ideas through as well," he pointed out Dan and Dave. "Even those crazy ideas that are only half-baked can lead to real breakthroughs," he added, noting that the IT team did not look enthusiastic about sharing their ideas any longer.

"We should probably get back to our stations," Nathan Riley, Thomas's deputy told the team diplomatically.

After reassuring himself that the new CEO was in fact leaving his department, Thomas Payne walked quietly back to his office. The members of the IT Department quickly resumed their normal tasks, but during breaks and lunch, there were some new discussions. The new CEO had kindled a small spark among the members.

# #2: QUIET CONFIDENCE

*Be calm and steady. Do not let your ego stand in the way of progress.*

---

**AT THE NEXT MEETING WITH** this executive team, Jay wanted to hit home another of his five traits: *quiet confidence*. Jay looked around at the C-Suite and said, "I want you to ask yourselves every day, are you letting your ego stand in the way?" He could tell that some of the executives were on board with this, but many others were not. Thomas Payne wasn't even looking in his direction or taking notes.

"With limited resources and declining profits every quarter, what do you suggest?" Josh Williams asked, hoping the new CEO would have answers that he didn't. Josh had come close to being terminated under the last two CEOs and didn't want to get off on the wrong foot with his new boss. He really was hoping Jay Admiral would have an answer.

"I don't have a magic cure for this organization," Jay told the C-Suite, "but I do know that every person in this organization needs to understand why they are here and what this organization does. In my visits to various work centers over the past week, I confirmed two things. One, the staff members do not know the vision, mission, themes, and goals for this organization. We can't expect to reach our goals if our staff members don't know what those goals are. Two, we have staff that have a lot of ideas and energy, but many are being stifled. We need to harness their ideas and innovations," Jay told his team.

"Do you want us to conduct a staff survey?" Dylan Jones, the Chief of Auditing asked the CEO.

"Not a bad start," Jay said. "We can solicit ideas from the staff and decide on projects that are easy and cost effective."

"What about my team's ideas of different ways to communicate to the staff?" Wendi Brown, the Chief of Marketing questioned. "Marketing studies show that people receive information in different ways. Some might respond well to the paper cards you suggested, but others might receive it better by e-mail or social media."

"I liked what I saw with the brainstorming session with your team. Let's develop a model of how we can communicate effectively to those at headquarters, where I see people every day, and those at branch offices, who might not be getting information directly or in a timely way."

"I'll need some help from the IT Department," his Chief of Marketing responded, looking pointedly at Thomas Payne.

Despite the fact that he hadn't appeared to be listening, Thomas Payne looked up. "My IT Department will support in any way we can."

"The next idea I have may not sit well with many of you, but this is important." He gestured to Martha to hand out lists to each of the executives. "I want suggestions for names from each of these sections to interact with me directly. I want a bio for each member being suggested, and there is only one rule for nominations." He paused and looked around the room, "The suggested member must be under age thirty."

"What?" Dylan Jones asked incredulously. "You want an advisory board of kids?"

"Some of these sections might not have anyone under thirty," Josh Williams commented, reviewing the list. "In those cases, do you want the youngest member of the current section?"

"Great point, Josh," Jay responded. "Please let me know which sections have no members under thirty, and we can decide the best solution on a case-by-case basis."

"Will do," Josh replied.

Jay looked at his executives and knew they weren't going to be happy. At least Dylan Jones, his Chief Auditing Officer, had expressed it out loud. "I know this is unusual, but what we have been doing isn't working. We don't have to take every suggestion from this board, but I am hoping they can generate some ideas that are unique and that those of us who are more mature wouldn't think of."

"You're the boss," Dylan said. "Just note that I for one am against it."

"I realize this is going to be challenging for some of you, but the second character trait is *quiet confidence*," Jay told his executive team. "I have confidence in each of you and your experience, but sometimes we as leaders need to be calm and steady. We need to put our egos aside and let junior members take the lead at times, not stand in the way of progress."

"Do you mean like a mentorship program?" Joyce Roberts, the head of Human Resources, who had been relatively quiet, asked.

"Not a formal mentorship program, Joyce," Jay responded, encouraged by her question. "More about supporting and developing others."

"Similar to on-the-job training," Josh stated.

"Yes," Jay agreed. "I want everyone to know that I appreciate your support and when we leave the executive team meetings, I expect that we leave here as a united leadership team and that even if you don't agree with the decisions made in this room, you support them."

"Either this will work, or we will all be looking for new jobs anyway," Dylan conceded. "The numbers have to come up, and we have tried almost everything else."

"It might actually be a way to attract younger members of the workforce to Regional Bank," Joyce agreed. "It also might help with the turnover and retention problem that you had me research."

There was some additional discussion, but most of the members agreed that the worst case would be a waste of time and couldn't harm the current financial situation. Jay noted that once again, Thomas Payne never voiced his opinion either way.

"Looks like we are making some progress," Jay told his executives and concluded the meeting.

# The Under-Thirty Board

**JAY HAD ALL THE BIOS** of his new under-thirty advisory board in his hand as he walked into the conference room. The staff members assembled around the table were not only much younger than the executives, but much more diverse. He had his assistants send out the agenda and some preparation material in advance, hoping to make progress on some of the issues facing the organization.

"You were each hand selected to represent various areas of Regional Bank," Jay said, diving right into the meeting. "I am optimistic that this group can provide some fresh perspective on some the challenges the bank is facing."

Jay looked around the room and could sense the energy around him as he continued. "Regional Bank has been in a steady decline for over a decade, and we are continuing to lose market share and profitability each quarter to our competitors. If we don't make some changes quickly and start seeing results, this organization won't survive." Jay didn't want to create panic, but he did want to convey the serious consequences of failure. He wasn't sure if the message of the troubles of the bank was making it to the junior staff members.

"Before I go any further, are there any questions?" Jay asked those assembled.

"How long do we have until the bank goes under?" Heather Whitmere, a teller from one of the suburban branches asked.

"According to the estimates I have seen," Park Wang, from Accounting responded, "the bank has about three years. It is most likely that the Board of Directors would sell the bank either in its entirety or in pieces first, though."

"That is on point, Park," Jay responded. "The board has given me one year to prove that Regional Bank can be turned around," he said, looking at the members to convey how serious the situation was for not only the organization, but to let it sink in regarding how it might impact them personally.

"We have been making suggestions for the past few years, but nobody wanted to implement our suggestions," Sean McDaniel from Operations stated. "Why will this time be any different?" he challenged Jay.

"I appreciate your question, Sean," Jay began, surprising some of the members around the table who weren't yet comfortable with challenging the CEO. Many were impressed that he also knew Sean by name. "As the new CEO with quite a few years left in my career, I need Regional Bank to be a success. I believe there are people in this room who have unexplored ideas that can be of value. I have an unwavering belief that we are stronger together, and that means everyone from the part-time teller at a branch to the Chairman of the Board of Directors."

"Can we share the financial situation of the bank with our colleagues?" Heather asked Jay.

"Yes, please do that in conjunction with our internal communications efforts. It is important that the messaging about the finances be focused on our need to improve and that this situation can be rectified," Jay responded. "I need everyone who works for Regional Bank to understand how serious our situation is and everyone's minds working on how we can improve things around here."

"I don't think most people outside of Accounting and Operations understand how grave the situation is," Sean commented.

"I hope you each had some time to review the materials that were sent in advance, because today I would like to start gathering your ideas and developing solutions," he told his new advisory board. "José Morales from Marketing had some ideas he wanted to present on how to improve communications between and among the staff," Jay said, handing the meeting over to José.

Jay was quiet during most of the meeting and observed that Ranjith Kumar from the IT Department didn't contribute unless directly asked a question. This concerned Jay as technology was essential for many of the ideas the rest of the team were suggesting. He hoped that as the team moved beyond the forming phase, Ranjith would open more to the group. Overall the meeting was positive, and there were a few initiatives that could be implemented quickly and at minimal cost. He looked to Dan and Dave from his Innovation Cell to work with the various members on their ideas and cultivate these new projects.

# First-Quarter Closing Preparation

---

**Josh Williams presented the first-quarter** closing results of the Regional Bank's branch offices with a smile for the first time in nearly two years. "All branches showed a slowing decline in market share, and profitability was almost identical to the previous year's first-quarter earnings. This may not appear to be good news," he said, looking around the room, "but for the first time in almost two years, the decline is slowing."

"That is very good news," Jay told his COO. He had been really impressed with Josh's work with the branches and his immediate changes that had led to the slowing of the decline in our branches.

"This has actually been the best quarter financially that we have had in the past nine," Bryson Adams, the Chief of Finance, interjected.

"I was skeptical of some of the methods proposed," Dylan Jones, the Chief of Auditing, admitted, "but it is hard to argue with results."

"The marketing team has been working closely with the under-thirty advisory panel, and we would like to make a few project proposals based on the successes we have seen this past quarter," Wendi Brown told the room. Jay had asked her to wait until the first-quarter results before requesting approval for projects that would require funding, no matter how small.

The executive board debated the prioritization of the projects proposed from the marketing team, but it was generally felt that most of the new initiatives would be worth the costs and that the risk was worth the potential rewards.

Jay again observed that his CIO, Thomas Payne, did not get involved in most of the conversation and appeared very reserved and distant. He responded to direct questions regarding the ability of his staff to support the projects and verified that the numbers that Ranjith Kumar had provided regarding outsourcing some of the IT appeared accurate.

"I would like to thank everyone for their efforts this past quarter," Jay told his executive team. "I would like to put out an internal newsletter to our employees to thank them for their efforts. I will also be going around to the work centers and to the branches as time permits in order to thank our staff members personally as much as possible."

"Can you stay behind a moment?" Jay asked Thomas as the executives left the meeting room.

"You have a concern about my IT Department?" Thomas asked Jay confrontationally.

"I need you on board with the direction that I am leading this team to include the IT department," Jay told his CIO. "IT is fundamental to the transformation and change that we need to improve our share in the marketplace."

"I have been telling everyone that for years," Thomas retorted.

"I know it is frustrating to not be listened to," Jay told Thomas. "Now that you are getting additional resources, the leadership of your team will be critical to our success."

"I understand," Thomas responded and walked out the door.

Jay hoped that his sidebar with Thomas would lead to change, but he recognized that not everybody would be on board with the changes he was making to the organizational culture.

# First-Quarter Board Meeting

---

**When Jay presented the first-quarter** results to the Regional Bank Board of Directors, he felt confident that they would be impressed with the numbers.

Howard Linton was the first to speak after the presentation. "Jay, I was somewhat skeptical when we brought you on board, but this is the first quarterly report we have had in a long time that didn't make me cringe." Derek voiced his support for the new CEO.

"I have to agree with you there," Brad Watts chimed in. "As everyone knows, I have been an advocate of selling off our assets before the bank loses any more value. This quarter is still a net loss," he continued, "but for the first time, the projections show a potential recovery of both market share and profitability."

"Does this mean we won't be fighting on that issue today?" Alice questioned Brad. "Such a shame as I have grown so fond of our verbal sparring on the matter." Alice sat flanked by her cousins Bert and Bart, who simply nodded. Bert was Josh's father and tried to remain as neutral as possible between his family members.

"I think with the increasing numbers, we could start shopping for a buyer or merger, Alice," Brad responded, increasing the tension in the room immediately and incurring dirty looks from all three Williams' family members.

"I can't believe I am going to say this," Alice countered, "but we gave Mister Admiral a year to meet market share and profitability numbers. After seeing the results this quarter, I am inclined to give him another three quarters."

"I know your family has been on this board for generations, Alice, but this is a financial investment for me, not a charity," Brad responded.

"Everyone was willing to forgo selling the assets, which is why we brought Jay on board," Howard pointed out. "I am also here to make a profit, but with the proposed ideas from Jay and his team and the current numbers, I would like to see how this plays out."

Travis leaned back in his chair at the head of the table and smiled at Jay. He had predicted how the various board members would respond to the quarterly report almost verbatim. After letting the conversation run its course for a while, Travis interjected, "Unless there is a movement for a vote on one of these proposals, I think it is time to adjourn this meeting." Everyone shook their heads indicating that there was no need to vote, and Travis closed the meeting.

"Do you have time for a cup of coffee?" Travis asked Jay.

"Of course." Jay smiled. "By the way, how are Molly and Hunter?"

"Great," Travis responded. "How are Lauren and the girls?"

"Doing well," Jay said, "But it's a lot quieter now that we are empty nesters."

Once they departed the building, Travis changed the topic back to the bank. "I have to be honest, Jay, when I first saw the numbers, I was surprised. You really accomplished more than I even I thought was possible."

"I am just providing some guidance and direction," Jay told Travis. "All of the ideas and implementation are coming from the existing staff. We are going to implement some new initiatives over the next quarter," Jay informed him.

"You know that even with one good quarter, the board won't approve any major projects," Travis cautioned him.

"All minor costs we can perform in-house or with minimal vendor support." Jay chuckled. "Next quarter, though, I will want to get some larger projects approved, and I was hoping you could start some behind-the-scenes networking to help," Jay confessed.

"If your numbers next quarter are this good, I think there is a fair chance depending on the cost–benefit and risk-versus-reward analysis," Travis paused as he opened the door to the coffee shop.

After ordering, the two men sat at an outside table, and the conversation turned to sports. As the two old friends debated which players deserved to be recognized and rewarded for their efforts, Jay had an idea. Jay left feeling optimistic about the future of Regional Bank.

# #3: CREATIVITY

*Always ask how you can do things better.*

---

**JAY LOOKED AROUND HIS OFFICE** at his administrative team and his innovation team. He was excited to see that members from the teams were sitting interspersed and that the conversation was flowing easily between those that Jay had brought over and the established members from the bank. Jay knew he had to get his team engaged and excited now that he had established a foundation during the first quarter.

"Today," Jay began, "we are kicking off our second quarter, and I am going to be asking the members in this room to start really tackling the third trait of true professional: *creativity*."

"I thought you hired us for our creativity," Dan joked while jabbing Dave in the ribs.

"That's true," Jay responded, "and the changes we have made have helped to slow down the decent, but now we need to move Regional Bank into an upward direction. That means we need to ask every day how we can do things better. I want to see crazy, wacky, and extreme ideas come forward. We won't be able to do them all, but we will be able to do some."

"Ideas have been coming in from most departments," Dave told Jay. "We are sorting through them and looking at the feasibility and chances for success."

"Which departments haven't responded?" Jay asked Dave.

"The IT Department most likely," Martha said under her breath.

Dave gave her a surprised look and responded, "The IT Department is actually the only one with no suggestions. I hadn't wanted to single them out."

"I appreciate your effort to be a team player, but sometimes I need to know the hard facts," Jay told Dave. "The IT Department is becoming an increasing concern."

"One reason why people might not be willing to share ideas is bad experiences from the past," he suggested. "We need to ensure that there are ways people can submit anonymously. They might feel that if their boss has already turned down the idea, they might get in trouble if they submit it directly to the top."

"Thanks for that feedback, Martha," Jay told her. "We need to have a culture of trust first in order for people to feel like they can share their creative ideas." Jay looked around the room. "Any creative suggestions on how to increase employee trust?"

"We used to have an employee-recognition program," Martha stated after a moment, "but I can't remember the last time anybody was recognized. I am sure I could get the old policy from Human Resources," she told him.

"That would be great," Jay said. "The sooner the better. I think it is time for us to start recognizing our team members again."

"Rob,"—Jay turned to his other assistant—"once we get a copy of the policy from HR, could you get the under-thirty board together? I think they will have some suggestions on how to modernize the program."

"Mister Admiral." Martha hesitated. He had told her to make suggestions, but this was still an unfamiliar area for her. "I think there are also a few senior members on the staff that might be of value to this effort."

Jay was pleasantly surprised that Martha had opened up to make another suggestion. She and Rob had started working together better and dividing tasks, but he could tell that she was still uncomfortable with the more progressive ideas he had and the open-door nature of his office. "Great," Jay said. "Work with Rob to have them at the meeting, and we can move forward with getting this kicked off. Besides recognition, any other suggestions?"

"I think the walk-throughs and open-door policy are working," Dave said. "The Marketing and Operations teams have been very responsive here at headquarters."

"Even the Human Resources and Auditing teams are starting to submit more ideas," Dan added, "but IT is still a very closed shop."

"We need to keep the ideas flowing in the headquarters," Jay agreed, "but don't forget about the branch offices. They are our face to the public." After a few more discussion points, the team wrapped up with a list of new ideas.

# Recognition Program

**The next morning when Jay** walked into the conference room and observed the members around the table, his smile broadened. The conference room was an integration of Millennials, Gen X, and Baby Boomers around the table; Jay appreciated the effort Martha and Rob must have put into getting this group together.

"It is great to have such a diverse group here today," Jay started. "It has come to my attention that there used to be a recognition program here at Regional Bank, but the program hasn't been in effect for a long time. I feel that recognizing the outstanding work and efforts of our team members is important. Martha and Rob shared a copy of the current recognition program with the group. It is my understanding that there are a lot of suggestions on how we can improve the program before implementing it," Jay concluded.

José Morales from Marketing was never shy and began, "Mister Admiral, this reward program is pretty old. Maybe we should just start over."

"Just because it is old, doesn't mean there isn't any relevance to it," Helen Gold from the HR Department responded. She was good friends with Martha, and Martha had encouraged her to speak up at the session. She had been around the organization a long time and didn't want to see the baby thrown out with the bath water.

"The reward structure actually makes a lot of sense, and the ability for supervisors to give small incentive rewards is good," Park Wang stated diplomatically.

"The rewards themselves have always been pretty terrible," Helen admitted honestly to the room. "When I was given my twenty-five years of service to the company award, my options were a man's watch or silver tie pin." She laughed.

Jay was surprised that in a business with so many women, the rewards didn't include more universal options. He was glad Helen was speaking up. He was enjoying the interaction between the various members in the room, and he wanted to break down some of the barriers between departments as well as generations.

"Some of the rewards are still relevant for the quarterly awards," Britney Johnson, the branch loan officer with whom Jay had first interacted, pointed out. "Time off and cash withstand the test of time." Britney's observation earned a few good-natured chuckles around the room.

"We could add some modern rewards as well," Ranjith Kumar, from IT added timidly. "We currently block social media sites, and employees could be rewarded with having those sites unblocked for half-hour periods so employees could check them during their lunch breaks. Since it is just a setting, there would be no additional expense to the organization, but a lot of people might appreciate it."

"That is a great idea," Helen said. "The only way I see pictures of my grandchildren is to go to the book of faces."

Ranjith beamed in response. He hadn't expected an advocate in the older woman.

"I like that you are thinking of low-cost options," Jay told the team and was pleased that Ranjith had decided to speak up at meeting. It was a good idea, and he wondered how many more ideas were locked away in Thomas Payne's IT Department.

"Parking spaces for those of us who work at headquarters is still good," Sean McDaniel from Operations said. "But there is no value to have a nice parking space at headquarters if you work in a branch office," he added.

"There aren't any team awards in the current policy," José Morales from marketing pointed out.

"That is an excellent point," Heather from the suburban branch agreed. "Even though it isn't official, there is already some competition between the branch offices. Maybe we could reward the branch with the highest quarterly goals with a free lunch."

"I like the idea of rewarding branches for meeting their quarterly targets," Jay agreed. "I don't know if I want it to be a competition, though. I think any branch that makes their quarterly targets should get the reward."

"Sort of like making the honor roll in high school," Heather said, "everyone who makes all As gets a reward, and it doesn't create animosity between branches."

"From an operations perspective, I think this will be great for morale. I can work with HR on getting this added to the policy," Sean McDaniel from Operations volunteered. "If a branch makes their quarterly targets, the price of lunch shouldn't be that much of an impact on the overall budget," he added.

Jay appreciated that the team members were all very conscious of the financial situation of Regional Bank and that the under-thirty members had freely been sharing this information. It had surprised Jay to find out that most of the staff had not been aware of the dire financial status of the organization when he started. Now he could see that his team was trying to make improvements with the understanding that there was a very tight budget.

"We could put together a similar information campaign to get the word out about the recognition program, as we are for the vision and mission," José Morales from Marketing suggested.

"I think we can have everything ready for approval in about two weeks," Helen Gold from HR said, going over her notes. "I will of course have to run it by Legal, but I don't see any red flags."

Jay was really impressed with how well the meeting went and felt that the new program would be good for morale. The team needed to know that he appreciated the effort they were putting into recovery efforts for the organization. Jay believed that it was essential to provide the team with knowledge, and that these efforts would lead to the success of the organization.

# Walk-Arounds

Jay knew that Dan and Dave were correct and that he needed to encourage each of the departments and branches to continue to share ideas. He also knew that he couldn't delegate all of the work to his team; he needed to continue meeting across the staff no matter how busy his schedule became.

# Midtown Branch Visit

**Over the next few weeks,** Jay spent time visiting the work centers and the branches to ensure that the team members understood the goals, vision, mission, and theme of the organization. One of his first stops was the midtown branch office at lunchtime. He was impressed with the changes as soon as he walked into the lobby. Every teller window was open and each teller engaged with a customer. He walked up to the back of the line, with only two people ahead of him.

"How long have you been waiting?" he asked the man in front of him.

"Just walked in the door," the stranger replied. "I used to hate coming to this bank. Sometimes it took my entire lunch hour and even made me late to get back. Not sure what changed, but over the past few months, it has improved to just a few minutes."

"Next," a teller called cheerfully.

"See what I mean?" The man laughed. "Excuse me." The two hadn't even noticed the that the other customer in line was already being served.

Jay noticed as a customer walked away and the teller looked over at Jay and smiled. Jay walked to the counter and was happy to see Jenn, the teller from his visit almost four months before. "Mister Admiral," she said, smiling, "Britney warned us you would be making surprise visits to the branches. We really appreciate the changes you have been making. Is there anything I can do for you?" she added.

Jay was amazed how the harried teller he had met four months prior had transformed into the cheerful woman in front of him. "I have a few questions for you," he told her, "but I don't want to hold up the line during rush hour. What time do things slow down for you here?"

"If you come back sometime between two o'clock and four o'clock, it should be pretty quiet, but many of the tellers will be on late lunch and some off around three because of the new hours you allow us to work."

"I'll be back around two o'clock, then," Jay told Jenn. As he walked out of the branch, he overheard two women discussing the service at the branch.

"I was coming in to close my account about two months ago, but the service was so good and the teller so kind that I ended up staying," she told her friend.

"I do almost all of my banking online," the other woman said.

"I just don't trust those machines, rather deal with a person," the first woman responded.

When Jay returned to the branch at two o'clock, he was greeted by enthusiastic staff who were excited to share their ideas with him. Mark, the branch manager, didn't want the spotlight and instead encouraged the tellers to talk directly with the CEO. The tellers explained how the new flexible work hours that had been established through the Operations and Human Resource staff had drastically changed the ability for tellers to cover peak hours and to reduce staff on the floor when the hours were not as busy. In addition, the flexible hours allowed tellers to arrange their schedules to support each other better to cover those attending college courses, as well all those with kids and other personal requirements. The flexible hours weren't just allowing better support for peak hours, Jay realized; they were adding to the team members' quality of life. Mark told Jay that Joyce in the head of Human

Resources had come to the branch twice to oversee the implementation and that the new practices would be standard for all the branches. Jay was glad to hear that both his COO and head of HR were working so closely on this initiative.

When Jay questioned the tellers about the goals, vision, mission, and themes, he was impressed with how well the tellers were able to explain these in their own words. One teller informed Jay, "The vision and goals are important. They let us know what our goals are, but the list of the traits of true professionals tells us how to do it."

"That is an interesting perspective," Jay acknowledged, "but can you explain why we need to do these things?"

"First, because if we don't change, the bank will go under, and we will all be out of jobs," she replied. "Second, vision is also the why. We are here to support our customers and meet their financial needs. When you look at it beyond a simple deposit or withdrawal, it is really about taking care of people."

Jay spent some time walking around the branch in between discussions with the team members and observed the physical changes to the branch. The break room had the posters displayed with the updated information. The screen savers on all the computers scrolled through the vision, mission, goals, themes, and traits as well. When he asked, a few of the team members even had their wallet-sized cards in their purses or tucked into a slot in their smart phone cases. Jay understood that to change the culture, he would need to continuously emphasize this information. One quarter of success would not change a culture that had been established for years. Jay was satisfied with the progress he was observing at the branch, but knew it was just a start.

When she was between customers, Jay stopped by Britney Johnson's office. "I was hoping to get a chance to speak with you while you are here at the branch," Britney said, giving him a genuine smile, nothing like the tight smile she gave him on their first meeting.

"It is nice to see your office so busy and customers leaving with smiles," Jay told Britney. "Josh, my Chief of Operations, has given me a lot of good reports about this branch.

"It has been like working in a new office since Josh has been working with Mark and allowing tailored changes to the loan program here," Britney responded. "Mark has always listened to our suggestions in the past. I don't think he had a good way to get these suggestions to corporate," Britney added, demonstrating her loyalty to her branch manager. "It is a real change to be empowered and to see the transformation across the branch."

"My goal is to see the transformation across the entire organization and not just the branch," Jay said.

"I think it is hard in the branches to feel like we are connected to the rest of the organization and to know what is going on across the other branches and at headquarters," Britney told him. "It seems like with today's technology, there should be better ways than a monthly newsletter to tell us what is going on."

"I have heard that from a few people, and the under-thirty board has brought it up a few times. The IT Department and Marketing Department are working on a few solutions," he told her.

"Things have changed a lot since you first came to this office, Mr. Admiral. I hope you know that we appreciate those changes and that our requests aren't ingratitude," Britney added.

"I don't have all the answers, and the changes in this organization take every member of the team," Jay responded. "When the team is all striving for the same goals, we can achieve more. We are stronger together."

# Marketing Department

JAY LOOKED FORWARD TO HIS visits to the Marketing Department. The team under Wendi Brown had been the first to embrace the new organizational concepts and were constantly embracing the trait of *creativity*.

Dan had informed Jay that the Marketing team was working with some start-ups on getting advertisements out to mobile platforms.

"How are you doing, Mister Admiral?" one of the marketing team members called out, spotting him as soon as he entered their work center.

"Today has been a fantastic day," Jay responded. "I just wanted to come by and see how things are going."

"We are pushing hard on the new external campaign about bringing service back to customers," José Morales chimed in.

"I visited one of our branches the other day," Jay told the Marketing team, who had started to gather around him. "The feedback I overheard from customers was very positive. Customer service has to be a cornerstone of what we provide to keep our current customers and attract new ones."

"We will also need to improve our online presence and customer service," Wendi Brown added, joining the group.

"I plan on bringing up the online banking issue at my next quarterly meeting with the Board of Directors," Jay informed Wendi. He also knew he needed to have a talk with his CIO about the project and wasn't looking forward to it.

# IT Department

**When Jay entered the IT** Department, Meg immediately sent an e-mail to Thomas Payne letting him know that the CEO was back in the basement. Thomas Payne looked at the e-mail in irritation and got up from his desk to see what the CEO was doing in his area again. His staff needed to focus on keeping servers running, not trying to impress the CEO with innovative thoughts.

Ranjith had become comfortable being on the under-thirty board and was introducing Jay to a co-worker who had some great ideas on apps and mobile platforms for the bank while maintaining cybersecurity. The IT Department was constantly arguing with Operations about customer service versus security, but luckily the legal experts always deferred to cybersecurity as there were too many public breaches and lawsuits to ignore. Ranjith and his teammate were explaining to Jay and the innovation leads that both customer service and cybersecurity were possible.

"Decided it was time to come disturb my IT Department again," Thomas said to Jay with a smile that didn't meet his eyes.

"I think it is important to get to know the team members and gather new ideas," Jay responded sanguinely.

"Your team has some great ideas," Dave told Thomas. "We have done a lot of research into the online banking options, and we would like to discuss putting a project team together to get the project off the ground."

Thomas was uncomfortable having this discussion in front of his staff. He felt that many were already becoming too emboldened with the CEO's new direction, and he preferred a more structured operation. "That would be fine," he responded. "Why don't we go into my office to discuss this."

"Great," Jay responded and followed his CIO into his office with Dave from his Innovation Cell.

Once seated, Jay began, "Research shows that we have to improve our online customer support services immediately to be competitive. I agree with your assessment that the internal staff is already spread too thin on keeping the antiquated legacy systems running, and that we need to outsource to a vendor. I would like the project manager to come from your team," Jay concluded.

Thomas had known that this request was coming from the executive meetings but had hoped to stall it for a few more months. "One of my best project managers is Pam Henderson," he told Jay.

"I will need you to distribute her current workload to the other IT project managers. We can't afford to hire any new staff right now," Jay told Thomas. "Will that be a significant problem?" Jay asked.

"We'll manage for now, but if I lose Nathan in addition to Pam, that would be catastrophic," Thomas told him.

"I understand," Jay told Thomas, understanding the constraints. "Right now, we are having to be very careful with our limited resources. When can you have Pam report?"

"I can have Pam available by early next week. Will you need any other support from my department?"

Jay had noticed that Thomas never prevented any projects or operations from happening but also never volunteered or suggested any new projects. He was not embracing the trait of *creativity*. "That should be all right now," Jay told him, "but I am sure this is just the beginning of what we will need to get the internal and external IT services where they should be."

Tom simply grunted in response.

"Can we step into your office a minute Thomas?" Jay asked the CIO.

"You're the boss," Thomas responded, clearly unhappy with the request.

Once inside Thomas's office with the door closed, Jay began, "I am concerned that you are not embracing the traits of true professionals and that work in the IT Department is suffering."

"My IT Department has been under funded for years," Thomas responded defensively.

"I agree with that," Jay told the CIO. "The lack of funding is being addressed as quickly as possible and within the budget constrained environment." Jay looked pointed at Thomas, "The lack of funding is not a reason for a lack of leadership, and I am concerned about this department."

"I understand," Thomas replied tersely. "Is that all?" he challenged Jay.

"It is all for now," Jay replied. "I hope to see some changes soon." Jay turned and left Thomas's office.

# The Bridge

**One night on the way** home from work, Jay was stuck in traffic on the 14$^{th}$ Street Bridge. He reflected on how the term *bridge* could have so many meanings. In this case, it was a physical structure that led between his office and the community where he lived. In the navy, the bridge was a physical space where the leader met with the team and communicated across the ship, and in larger cases the battle group of ships. Metaphorically, bridges are what allow different entities to connect.

The more Jay thought about the concept of bridges, the more he was convinced that this was the solution to the internal communications problems across Regional Bank. Britney's comment about the branches not feeling connected to the headquarters had hit home. Jay asked Martha to send a quick note to Wendi on his idea and asked her to schedule a meeting with his Marketing, Admin, and Innovation teams at the first available opportunity.

The next morning, Wendi and her team were excitedly discussing how to create a virtual bridge for Jay. "I think we have to look at this the same as we do external marketing," Wendi told her teammates.

"Some people still want the old print monthly newsletters," José said in disbelief, "but what if we rebrand ours *The Bridge*?"

"I like that," Dave said. "Give people what they are familiar with, but at the same time, modernize."

"We could also start using social media like a restricted group on the book of faces," Wendi added.

"Jay and our innovation team has used Flitter in the past," Dan suggested.

"We could also leverage the existing internal website. Ranjith mentioned that there is a blog feature that we don't use," José told the group.

"Between the Admin team and the Marketing team, we can coordinate the messaging so that the newsletter, blog posts, and social media all have similar content and branding but also are tailored for each audience," Rob suggested.

"Is it better to stagger the messaging or put it all out at the same time?" Martha questioned.

"I think it depends on the message," Wendi said, "For a major announcement, we might want to use everything available at once, but for consistent messaging, we may want to stagger the message throughout the month."

"Hey," Rob said, "I know this is pretty basic, but we haven't talked about e-mail yet."

"We will also want to ensure we are looking at themes and messaging," Dan pointed out.

After about an hour, the team felt that they had a solid communications plan to present to Jay. He needed to be able to communicate across the bank both at the headquarters to the branches and at all levels. *The Bridge* was forming!

# Second-Quarter Closing Preparation

**Jay looked at the team** assembled in his office. "I want to thank all of you for your extra effort to ensure that the online banking system proposal is ready for the board."

"We couldn't have done it without all the members of the team working together," Dan told Jay and smiled at those in the office.

"We have put our best offering together, and I know that it is being seriously considered," Jay agreed. "The efforts everyone has taken across the bank at every level and each office has helped to improve our market share and slow our decline."

"We are using *The Bridge* to communicate this to the team," Wendi responded. "Understanding the severity of our financial situation has helped to galvanize everyone."

"Yes," Martha agreed enthusiastically, "from the tellers—I mean customer service representatives—to the department heads."

"I think there is actually a chance the project will get approved," Josh said. "I know that my sources say that the increasing numbers are in our favor."

# SECOND-QUARTER BOARD MEETING

---

"SO," ALICE WILLIAMS RAISED A skeptical eyebrow at Jay, "based on a one-percentage-point increase in profitability and a flat market share, you want us to invest in an online banking system?"

"Sometimes you have to spend money to make money," Howard interjected. He had found Jay's proposal to be compelling and liked the concept of agile development.

"The vendor does have a great reputation, and the price is very competitive," Brad added. "If we want to raise the value of this bank, we have to offer modern banking solutions."

"What about the security of this proposed solution?" Alice argued. "I thought we had decided on the current solution to ensure we weren't going to end up on the cover a newspaper with a headline saying that we were hacked."

"The vendor and our internal IT Department will be working together on secure solutions that meet the strictest regulations, and you know Dylan in Auditing will be ensuring strict compliance with regulations," Jay added.

"Jay has already had more success than I expected with the brick-and-mortar operational changes," Brad told the board. "I think we need to give him a chance."

"When you look at the one-percent increase in profitability, we are spending almost exactly that on Jay's proposed project," Derek pointed out. "Jay has actually earned the project through his work the past six months. Even if we agree to this expenditure, we are still better off than we were in our continuing downward trend."

"I would like to call for a vote," Brad told the board.

"Second," Howard said.

"All in favor of approving the expenditures for the online banking system," Travis called. The vote passed, and Jay was ready to start on his first funded project at Regional Bank.

# #4: TEAMWORK AND COLLABORATION

*No one person is smarter than the entire organization working together.*

---

JAY KNEW THAT THE NEW online banking project was going to have an impact across the bank, so he started his next executive meeting with a focus on the fourth character trait of true professionals. "*Teamwork and Collaboration* are essential to the success of this organization. No one person is smarter than the entire organization working together," he told his executive team.

"The online banking project will be our number-one project over the next quarter," Jay continued. "I expect every department to pitch in when needed.

Pam Hendersen is the lead from our IT team, and she has put together a list of who she needs on the team and the approximate number of hours she estimates they will need to be dedicated to the project."

"I can support this," Wendi said with enthusiasm when she received the project resource list.

"My team understands that this is the bank's number-one effort," Josh told the table. "We have needed to do this for a long time, and it might be what saves this bank," he added.

"I will do my best to make sure that none of the new applications break the current systems or cause any additional cybersecurity vulnerabilities," Thomas said. "I still have concerns that my best project manager is gone, and we barely hold the place together with our current staff."

Jay recognized that this was not exactly a glowing endorsement to support the project, but was the most that had been volunteered from his CIO.

# CHANGE OF VENUE

---

**MARTHA WAS FRUSTRATED AND BESIDE** herself. She immediately went to Rob for his suggestions. "The auditorium and conference rooms we booked for Mister Admiral's offsite are flooded," she told Rob. "The manager called and said there is no way we can hold our offsite there in two days; the water mains burst."

To celebrate the success of the past six months and to provide a single face-to-face meeting with all the team members at Regional Bank, Jay had requested that a half-day offsite be held on a Saturday after hours. The board and been reluctant, but when faced with the Q2 results, they had approved a modest sum for the facility rental and allowed for compensation time off for hourly employees; overtime wasn't in the current budget. Rob and Martha had found a terrific venue that was within their small budget, but now it was literally under water.

"I guess we need to start making calls to other venues," Rob responded stoically, knowing that finding another venue the day before the event with their budget would be next to impossible.

Martha smiled at Rob and said, "*Quiet confidence.* We'll find something."

Rob flashed her a brilliant smile in return. "I'll start calling venues from the back of the alphabet, and you start with the front."

"Agreed," Martha replied. Her reminder to Rob to be calm and steady also helped her to do the same.

For several hours, they made no progress. Dan came in and saw the two assistants looking worn. "Anything I can do?" he asked.

"We have tried everything we can think of, Dan. Hotels, conference facilities, even some banquet halls. We only have a day and half to find a large-enough venue within our price range on a Saturday afternoon."

"Give me the details on how many rooms and the number of people we need to accommodate," Dan told Martha and Rob. "I might have an idea."

About thirty minutes later, Dan and Dave came back into the room, where Rob and Martha were still desperately trying come up with a venue. Dan and Dave announced, with big smiles and high fives, "We found a new venue." They told their teammates, "We will need to get the new address out as soon as possible to the staff. Some may have already gone home for the day."

"Wendi's team in Marketing has really become experts on communicating with the staff on multiple forms of media," Rob mentioned. "I guess it is time for us to put *The Bridge* to the test."

After getting ahold of the Marketing and Human Resource teams to get the change of venue out to the staff, the four decided to call Jay with the news about the flooded hotel and the new venue.

Martha reflected on how they had been able to use the character traits of true professionals throughout the minor crisis. She had worked on many other teams where civility would have been severely strained under the circumstances. Two of the past CEOS had commonly cursed at Martha when travel plans were changed duc to weather. She couldn't imagine what profanities they would have unleashed on her in a situation like this. Martha was proud to call these members her new teammates and despite some initial misgivings about the new venue, she thought it certainly showed creativity!

# THE RING

**ON SATURDAY AFTERNOON, SEVERAL MEMBERS** of Regional Bank looked mildly perplexed as they were pulling into an old boxing arena. Many people were double-checking the address on their smart phones. On the billboard in bright letters, "Regional Bank" was clearly emblazoned for all to see.

"Glad you got the change of venue." Staff members were greeted as they entered the arena. Some of them were giddy, and others giggled nervously as they entered.

The department heads stood around a table getting briefed by Martha on the new locations of their breakout sessions. The plan was to use conference rooms in the old venues, but now they were improvising with training rooms and other facilities for each of the departments.

"Ideally, we don't end up in a locker room," Josh quipped with Wendi.

"I think this is much more fun than it would have been in the conference center," Wendi told him. "This feels much more energetic."

Dylan from Auditing joined his fellow executives and surprised them by saying, "Wendi, I have to agree. I was dreading the offsite, but who can't get at least a little excited about going to a sports venue?"

"I think we should have cancelled the entire event," Thomas Payne muttered under his breath.

As the executives left the table where Martha had briefed them and headed into the arena, they could hear that the venue was abuzz. This was certainly the most exciting vibe before any speech from a CEO that they had ever attended.

Rob had volunteered to introduce Jay and decided to capitalize on the venue and introduce his boss like a boxer. "Ladies and gentlemen," he began in his best sports announcer voice. "For today's main event in the center ring, I bring to you former Naval Academy boxer and the reigning CEO of Regional Bank: Jaaaaaay Admiraaaal!"

Jay walked into the ring with a thunderous applause from his staff. "I hope I can live up to that wonderful introduction," Jay told the crowd. "I want to start by thanking the team that has put this offsite together and for the flexibility everyone has shown by being here today. Regional Bank has been struggling for several years, but in the past six months, we have started to turn that around." Jay paused and looked around the room. "The effort of each person in this room is what has changed the bank. I want you to thank the person sitting next to you for their efforts." Jay heard a few murmurs but knew his staff could do better. "Congratulate them like they just won in this ring," he told the staff. He could now hear people loudly congratulating teammates and giving shout-outs. He let this continue for a few minutes, prowling around the boxing ring and observing his staff.

"There have been a lot of changes at Regional Bank over the past six months, and change can be hard," he paused, circling the ring. "I have watched as the members of this organization embraced the vision and mission, understanding that a failure by one is a failure to all and that without change, Regional Bank won't be around much longer," he paused again, to let this point sink in. "It is with your efforts and innovation the bank has shown a profit for the first time in many years."

A few members clapped at that statement. "That's the best you got?" Rob called from the side of the ring, and the arena burst into applause.

Jay waited again for the crowd to quiet down before resuming. "Six months ago, I challenged each of you to demonstrate and live by the Character Traits of True Professionals, and I have not been disappointed. I have watched as team members have shown their support to others, demonstrating *civility*. I have observed staff set aside their egos to ensure project success and show *quiet confidence*. This team has overwhelmed me with suggestions, and we have achieved goals others thought were not possible with our *creativity*. I have many examples of *teamwork & collaboration*, to include the team that put this venue together at the last minute." That comment earned a few whoops from the audience, and Jay let the energy flow. "Finally, I am proud that we do everything we do showing *honesty & integrity*, because without this trait, there would be no confidence in us as a banking institution."

Jay circled the ring, looking at various members of the audience, and added, "But we are only at the halfway point, and there is more work that needs to be done. I heard from many of the branches that they felt disconnected from the headquarters, so I wanted to include everyone possible at this event." That earned him a few cheers from the audience. "I am going to ask a lot of you," he told the staff. "I am going to push each one of you to reach our goals and to make Regional Bank exceptional again, a place you are proud to work at." Jay paused. "More importantly, a place you are proud to bank at." The crowd cheered, and Jay felt more like he was at a pep rally than an all-hands and appreciated how the venue had helped to set the tone.

"In a little while, we will have breakout sessions, where you can talk to the different executives about the way ahead for our organization and what exciting projects and changes you will see over the next six months. We have training rooms and other facilities available. There have been e-mails and tweets containing the floor plan and department locations. If you aren't sure where you need to go, please see one of the offsite planning team members at the registration area," Jay told the members.

"Before I release you to the breakout sessions, I would like to open up the floor for any questions. Please stand and come up to the front, where two of my team members are available with microphones so everyone can hear." The crowd was excited. It was the first time that a CEO of Regional Bank had opened the floor to questions at an all-hands.

One of the Customer Service Representatives from the suburban office approached a microphone. "The tellers in my branch, but I think others, too," she began nervously, "find it frustrating that the branch managers are often hired externally and that there is not career progression to go to headquarters or another part of the bank. Would it be possible for HR to consider putting a career progression program in place?"

"That is an area I'm not familiar with," Jay told her honestly. "I will take a note to look into this, and if you could leave your name and contact information with one of my assistants, I will get back with you personally."

The next member waiting for a microphone came from Auditing. "Thank you for taking the time to listen to us directly," Park Wang told the CEO. "I would like to thank you for letting me be a member of the under-thirty advisory board, but was wondering what is the future of the board?"

"Thanks for that question, Park," Jay responded. "For as long as I am the CEO, I plan on keeping the advisory board in place and rotating members on an annual basis to keep it fresh and open to new ideas."

Next, a member from IT asked a question. "If Regional Bank is sold at the end of the year, what happens to our jobs?" This question brought a loud murmur from the crowd as many people had the same thought but had been afraid to ask.

"My goal," Jay responded, "is to ensure that Regional Bank stays in place and that we have a successful future. I don't view failure as an option, and I hope the successes of the past six months helps to inspire each of you in achieving our goals."

"I understand that everyone has different financial and home life situations they need to consider, and maybe the bank won't be a good fit for them in future. If you are concerned about your specific situation, I encourage you to talk to your supervisor or a member of Human Resources. You can also ask me directly through the multiple communications channels through *The Bridge* or take advantage of my open-door policy and come by my office," Jay encouraged the crowd.

Jay concluded, "I am optimistic about the future of Regional Bank and urge each of you to do your part, as we are Stronger Together."

With that, Jay concluded the questions, and each executive held a session on the specific goals for their teams over the next two quarters. Jay poked his head into many of the training areas and was impressed with the teamwork and collaboration taking place.

# Online Banking IT Project

---

**Jay asked his Chief of** Marketing and Chief of Information to stop by the online banking IT project management meeting to congratulate the team on their early successes. The three entered the room from behind Pam as she was speaking.

"I would like to thank everyone who has made this project a success so far," Pam told her team. "I really appreciate the partnership with our vendor team and the efforts of our Marketing team to get the message out about our new services." Pam's team was using agile project management and was churning out a new development every three weeks. Positive feedback from customers had been coming in the past few weeks.

"I would like to thank everyone for their hard work as well," Jay said, stepping forward with his two executives. The board was nervous about approving the funding for this project, as you are all aware, and these early successes are already showing an impact on the bottom line."

The people in the room cheered, and Pam added, "Thank you so much, Mister Admiral. The team has been so amazing, and the spiral development has gone even better than anticipated. Even the cyber security team members and lawyers have been approving our work quickly."

"I hope the work this team is doing will provide us the ability to reward you the way you deserve in the future, but under the current financial constraints, we wanted to show you our appreciation. We know it isn't much," Wendi said, "but we have brought some donuts for your hard-working team." She presented the box of sugary pastries to Pam, who handed the box around the table.

"It really has been the efforts of José and the Marketing team who have made all the difference," Pam said humbly. "Also, the leadership from Dave and the assistance from the innovation team have been invaluable," she added to Mr. Admiral.

"Well, from what you just said, it sounds like all the other team members are doing the work," Thomas told Pam. "It sounds like you aren't doing much."

Pam stood awkwardly in front of the room, her face red, and didn't respond to the comment from her boss. Such comments were typical in the IT Department.

"Without Pam, we would be a motley crew," José from Marketing immediately defended his project manager.

"Pam takes care of all the resourcing so the rest of us can focus on the details," another team member added protectively.

"Pam is just giving us the credit for the work she does," another member piled on.

"The project success we have had so far is due to Pam and the entire team," Jay said seriously. "Regional Bank needs this project to continue its recent market increases and profitability."

Jay was impressed with how Pam's team members rallied around their leader but knew that the situation with his CIO couldn't continue much longer. He was glad Pam's team members had rallied around her, but once again, Thomas had scorned the trait of *civility*.

# Third-Quarter Closing Preparation

"**THE ONLINE BANKING PROJECT IS** on track, and we are increasing both our market share and profit," Rob told Jay in preparation for the third quarter board meeting.

"This is by far the smoothest that this bank has run in over a decade," Martha told her boss.

"For the first time," Jay told this staff, "I don't feel like I am walking into the lion's den instead of a board room."

# THIRD-QUARTER BOARD MEETING

---

**"I HAVE TO SAY I** am mildly impressed," Alice told the board room. "We have experienced both an increase in profitability and market share this quarter."

"I would go beyond mildly impressed," Brad countered. "The markets are in a wait status and advising shareholders to hold instead of sell stock in Regional Bank. This is great news."

"Jay is asking for additional funds for online banking and cyber security," Travis pointed out to the board. "Do we need to have further discussion, or are we ready to vote?" He could feel the consensus in the air and was hoping for a short meeting. It was rare for Alice and Brad to be on the same side.

"I move for a vote," Howard said.

"Second," Brad called out.

"All in favor?" Travis was happy to accept the unanimous vote and calling the meeting to a quick close.

"Congratulations," Travis told Jay on the way out the door. "You really are a miracle worker."

"Do you have a few minutes for coffee?" Jay asked Travis. "There is a concern I have about a member of the executive team that I would like to discuss with you."

"Certainly," Travis said, and he and Jay headed to one of their favorite coffee shops.

# #5: HONESTY AND INTEGRITY

*Never violate the law or regulations; tell the truth unflinchingly.*

---

JAY KNEW THAT *HONESTY & integrity* were the cornerstone of character and that in order to live by the Character Traits of True Professionals, he had to confront an issue he had observed over the previous nine months. Integrity is about doing right thing, no matter what, not about simply following the rules.

# Talking Things Through

**That night, Jay went home** to Lauren with a weary expression she hadn't seen in many years. She could tell that Jay needed to talk about his work situation. "The numbers are looking better for Regional Bank in the stock market," Lauren opened, sure that wasn't what was bothering her husband.

"Yes, they really are," Jay responded, "but I am having some difficulty with one of the executive team members. I guess I am bringing my work home to you," he smiled softly at his wife who gave him the strength to go to work each day.

"Tell me about the situation," Lauren encouraged him.

Jay explained to Lauren that one of his executive team didn't appear to be on board with the Character Traits of True Professionals and that he was lacking in at least three of the five areas to include being kind to others as part of civility. While explaining the lack of creativity and improvement in the IT Department and other concerns, Jay felt a sense of relief to be able to discuss the situation.

When Jay was done describing the situation, Lauren told him, "Jay, you have lived by your Character Traits of True Professionals for a long time, and that is one of the reasons why I am always so supportive of you. One of those traits, *honesty and integrity*, is about telling the unflinching truth. Have you talked to this direct report yet about your concerns?"

Jay knew Lauren had hit the nail on the proverbial head. He had hoped that Thomas would come around, and since Thomas avoided direct conflict and did enough to get by, he hadn't had a direct conversation with him about his concerns. Jay needed to schedule a private meeting with Thomas to discuss his observations and how the CIO had failed to meet his expectations.

"Thanks for always being there with me to talk through the tough issues, Lauren," Jay told his wife.

"Jay," she responded, "you know I can always tell when you are struggling, and most of the time it is because you are having a small conflict with adhering to your own True Traits. Sometimes everyone needs to talk through their problems."

Jay kissed his wife gently. "This is what makes you my best teammate," he told her sincerely.

# Live by Your Word

**Jay asked his support team** to schedule a private meeting in his office with the CIO. Despite the many opportunities he had given Thomas, he simply wasn't adjusting to the new ways of doing business at Regional Bank or embracing the Character Traits of True Professionals.

Thomas wasn't surprised by the meeting invitation. If anything, he was surprised at how long it had taken Jay to schedule the inevitable. Thomas walked into Jay's office and said, "Jay, nice office you have up here. I'm surprised you get down to the basement as often as you do with these plush leather chairs." Thomas realized this was the first time he had been in the office since the current CEO had taken over the bank.

"Thanks for coming by," Jay told Thomas.

"Did I have a choice?" Thomas responded. Thomas had a reputation for being sarcastic and even snarky to his direct reports, and Jay had witnessed this behavior himself at the celebration for the online banking team before the third quarter board meeting.

"Are you happy here?" Jay asked Thomas, catching the CIO somewhat off guard by the question.

"I'm not sure what you mean," Thomas responded. "I worked my way through the IT ranks to become the CIO and now I have a job that pays the bills. I have never really considered whether or not I should be happy at work."

"You are in a leadership role, Thomas," Jay told the CIO. "As leaders, we need to be able to inspire our followers, especially in the type of financial situation that Regional Bank is in right now."

"I have focused on ensuring that Regional Bank has the best possible IT support our budget allows," Thomas responded defensively.

"You are focused on the technology and not the people," Jay responded gently.

"I would have to agree with you there," Thomas said. "I have always enjoyed the tech more. Technology works great until people screw it up."

"I find that people perform best when they are in positions and jobs that inspire them. You don't appear to be inspired by the mission and vision of Regional Bank, and I am very concerned that you haven't embraced the Character Traits of True Professionals," Jay told the CIO.

"That," Thomas responded, "I thought those were just gimmicks to get the rank and file to follow you. To be honest, I haven't been comfortable with a lot of the changes that you have been making and the amount of direct interaction with my staff."

"Have you thought about where you would be if you weren't at Regional Bank?" Jay asked Thomas.

"I am pretty close to retirement," Thomas told Jay. "For the right severance package, I would be willing to go a bit early and get some extra tee time in at the golf course."

Based on Jay's conversation with Travis, this is the direction he had been hoping Thomas would go. "I think it might be a good opportunity for us to call Joyce in from HR and discuss the options."

After a few days of negotiations and paperwork, Thomas accepted an early retirement package, and Nathan, his deputy, became the next CIO at Regional Bank. Jay was relieved that Thomas had left quietly, and he had been impressed with Nathan the previous few months.

# Do the Right Thing

**"CAN I GET IN TO** see Jay as soon as possible?" Wendi asked Martha on the phone.

"I can fit you in, in about half an hour," Martha responded, reviewing Jay's schedule and hearing the urgency in Wendi's voice. "Should I invite anyone else to the meeting?"

"Please invite someone from Legal…and Dave and Dan please," Wendi responded, then added, "Oh, and Josh from Ops and Nathan from IT as optional." There had been a time that it wouldn't have occurred to her to add so many people, but Jay's value of *teamwork and collaboration* had changed how meetings were conducted in the organization.

Thirty minutes later, they were all gathered in one of the conference rooms. Wendi opened the meeting, "One of our competitors has had a serious security breach. There are a few different ways we could approach this from a marketing standpoint, and I would like get some thoughts."

Josh was the first to speak. "We have been promoting our new web and mobile applications as secure, and I know that Nathan's team has been working overtime to ensure the security as Pam and the vendors are conducting each spiral."

"I don't like the idea of capitalizing on the misfortune of one of our competitors," Jay told his team. "It doesn't feel ethical, and it could be us next time."

"I agree," Josh said, "but I think keeping our current campaign highlights that we have built cyber security into our systems as we have been rolling them out."

"Since we have been marketing that our systems have security built in from the inception, it might be a good idea to have an independent assessment," Nathan told the team. "It would be really bad if we were breached after promoting ourselves as a bank with strong cybersecurity. I have brought Kevin Carpenter, my cybersecurity lead here who agrees that we should ensure we are not vulnerable to a similar attack." Nathan added.

"That's great thinking, Nathan," Jay told his new CIO. Let's also pull in Sandy Taylor and see if the Auditing team has any insights. I agree the assessment needs to come from an external source."

"I know we have agreed to not exploit this issue, but would there be value in letting our current customers know that because of recent cyber security threats we are reviewing our posture and conducting additional testing to ensure that our systems are safe?" Wendi asked the group.

"A lot of my friends have been slow to move to mobile applications because they don't think these apps are secure," Martha told the team. "I think it would help to give our existing customers peace of mind."

"I agree with reassuring our existing customer base," Jay told the team. "We have been making a lot of progress in this area and don't want to lose the customers we have gained."

"I am anticipating that the press will be contacting us about our cybersecurity here at Regional Bank," Wendi told the team. "I will draft a press release based on this morning's discussion and get it out for review to all the departments. Nathan," she added, "it would really help to get a member of the cyber team to help with the drafting of the statement."

"I will send someone up to your department right away," Nathan told Wendi. Nathan was enthusiastic about being a part of executive team and finding that his members were adding value across the organization.

"It is good to see you included your security lead and other team members," Jay told Nathan, knowing that Thomas would never have included this staff members.

"The team was handpicked by Kevin," Nathan said differing to his cybersecurity lead.

"Pride prevents progress," Kevin told the group, embodying the trait quiet confidence. "We need to have our best experts in house and call in reinforcements to ensure that we are as secure as possible."

"Glad to have the support of the entire IT Team," Jay told the group.

"I am glad you approve of the changes I am making," Nathan replied humbly. "I realize that he IT Department needs to embrace the Traits of True Professionals."

"Thanks for getting everyone together to tackle this issue, Wendi," Jay told his Chief of Marketing. "We are always stronger together."

# One Year Review Closing Preparation

---

**Jay and the team reviewed** the numbers one final time, and everyone looked slightly defeated. "We are close," Jay told his team. "We did our best, and the final decision will up to the board."

"After the entire bank has pulled together, you would think we would have made it," Martha said, disappointed."

"You did a lot to help us get the staff on board," Rob told Martha sincerely.

"Everyone has pulled together over the past year," Josh told the group. "Don't give up yet."

"I know I am coming in tomorrow like we will be in business forever," Wendi told the group with a smile and enthusiasm.

"Wendi, you always stay so upbeat," Dave said, catching her infectious smile.

"I'll let everyone know the results from the board as soon as I am done," Jay told the team. "In the meantime, Wendi is right: there is a lot of work to do."

# One Year Board Review

**Alice Williams looked at Jay** sternly. "I didn't want to bring you on board as the CEO," she said bluntly. "After a review of the metrics we gave you to meet, you are still a full percentage point lower from meeting the profitability goals and almost two percentage points below the market share that we asked you to obtain."

"That's correct," Howard cut in, "but I never expected Jay to get this close to begin with; the goals were stretch goals."

"Despite not hitting the exact numbers, Jay has transformed Regional Bank, and his success over this past year is an indication we should keep him on board," Travis told the other members of the board.

"The numbers are impressive, and currently the market predictions are that if we stick with Jay, shareholder values will continue to increase," Brad told the table. "For the first time in years, experts are recommending that consumers buy Regional Bank stock."

"Does that mean that for the first time in years, you aren't going to try to convince this board to sell the bank off in pieces or for a fraction of its worth?" Alice sniped at Brad.

"Jay didn't make his numbers, but I think we should keep him as CEO," Howard told the board.

"I can't believe this, but I am agreeing with Howard," Brad told the table. "If we switch CEOs again, it won't be a good message to the shareholders."

"Jay has earned the respect of the employees and the shareholders," Bert Williams spoke up uncharacteristically. "I support keeping the bank in one piece and renewing Jay for another year." A few murmurs could be heard around the room at Bert's decisive statement.

"Is that a call for a vote?" Travis asked Bert.

"Yes," Bert said.

"Seconded," Bart followed without being called on.

"The vote on the floor is to keep Regional Bank intact and to keep Jay Admiral in the role of CEO for one additional year," Travis told the board. "All in favor?"

The board voted unanimously in favor, despite Jay being a few percentage points off his goals.

# #6: DETERMINATION

---

**JAY WALKED INTO HIS OFFICE** and added a sixth trait under the Character Traits of True Professionals: *#6 Determination: Never, never, never give up*! Jay had realized during the board meeting that this was the trait that drove him throughout his career and would continue to guide him both at Regional Bank and beyond.

“Can you update the Character Traits of True Professionals with a sixth trait?” Jay asked his staff.

“Sure thing, boss,” Rob responded with a smile looking at the board.

“Already messaging our internal web team,” Martha told him.

“Guess I’ll call the printer,” Rob laughed.

“Wait until tomorrow, when I can get with the team and we can develop our new targets and metrics,” Jay said with a smile.

# Good Night

**THAT NIGHT WHEN JAY WENT** home, he told Lauren that he added a sixth trait. Lauren smiled and said, "That has always been there. You just never wrote it down before."

"Thanks for agreeing to taking on this project with me a year ago," Jay told his wife.

Lauren smiled. "I accepted that life would be a project with you many years ago, Jay."

"You are the only person whom I would want to share my life as a project with," Jay joked back.

Lauren laughed. "What did you do with that thrift store suit you bought to do your own investigation into the customer service at Regional Bank?"

"Saving it for whatever comes next," he told her. "I plan on training Josh Williams to take on the role of CEO one day, and then I will need something else to do."

"Never give up," she whispered and gave her husband a hug.

# CHARACTER TRAITS OF TRUE PROFESSIONALS

## #1: CIVILITY

*Be kind, share credit, and maintain your sense of humor! Don't lose your temper.*

---

## #2: QUIET CONFIDENCE

*Be calm and steady. Do not let your ego stand in the way of progress.*

---

## #3: CREATIVITY

*Always ask how you can do things better.*

---

## #4: TEAMWORK & COLLABORATION

*No one person is smarter than the entire organization working together.*

---

## #5: HONESTY & INTEGRITY

*Never violate the law or regulations; tell the truth unflinchingly.*

---

## #6: DETERMINATION

*Never, never, never give up!*

# Author's Notes

**I HAD THE PRIVILEGE TO** serve as a government civilian under Admiral James Stavridis while he was the North Atlantic Treaty Organization (NATO) Supreme Allied Commander Europe (SACEUR) and US European Command Commander (EUCOM). While serving under Stavridis, I truly understood what Jim Collins meant in *Good to Great* about leaders creating a cult-like culture.

When I returned to the US European Command several years later, many things had changed, but the references to Stavridis's Character Traits of True

Professionals lingered. It was during this time that I wrote my first book, *The Project Manager: Life is a Project*, and conceived of the idea for this book.

My old boss and good friend Stephen Ewell provided an e-introduction to James Stavridis, who has been wonderful and far more responsive than I deserve. Writing in the genre of leadership fables, I wanted to move the Character Traits of True Professionals out of the military environment and show their applicability to all professional environments.

Jay Admiral's timeline is counterfactual based on the musings of Admiral Stavridis in *The Accidental Admiral* when he considered leaving the US Navy. Using the books written by Admiral Stavridis, reminiscences from my coworkers, and my own research, I hope that the character of Jay Admiral is as inspiring and educational as the man himself.

I would like to thank my sister, Barbara Madison, who provided significant context for the banking environment. Her experience in the banking industry has helped me attempt to create a realistic world. Any accuracy is her part, and any shortcomings are mine.

I reworked this entire book in a cabin in Westcliffe, Colorado, belonging to my good friends Michael and Michelle Mras (of course it was my cabin first). Michelle fell in love with the cabin as a place to write, and it is truly an author's refuge. Inspired by Michelle and her incredible passion and zeal for life, writing has flowed the past week. Please take a moment to check out Michelle's works *Eat, Drink, and be Mary* and *It's Not Luck: Overcoming You.*

# ACKNOWLEDGMENTS

**I WOULD LIKE TO THANK** the countless people who have assisted me in writing this book.

My test readers have been incredible and I appreciate the patience of Christopher Durham, Charles Hulse, Barbara Madison, and Robert Watson along with their great feedback.

I would like to thank James Woosley from Free Agent Press and Jennifer Harshman from Harshman Services for always being there for me and helping me to reach the end point.

I would like to thank all those that have served; especially those that were with me serving under Admiral Stavridis at the US European Command.

# About the Author

**Amy S. Hamilton** is a cyber security professional, IT project manager, author, motivational speaker, and shoe aficionado. She became a certified Project Management Professional through the Project Management Institute in 2007 and has been a volunteer in her local chapters in Stuttgart, Germany and Colorado Springs, CO. She presented on the "The Secret to Life from a PMP" at TEDxStuttgart in September 2016. She taught Project Management Tools at Colorado Technical University and was a facilitator for the Master's Degree Program in Project Management for Boston University.

Amy holds a Bachelor of Science (BS) in Geography, from Eastern Michigan University, a Master of Science (MS) in Urban Studies from Georgia State University, Master in Computer Science (MSc) from the University of Liverpool, Master Certificate in Project Management (PM) and Chief Information Officer (CIO) from the National Defense University, and completed the US Air University, Air War College. She is a Doctor of Philosophy (PhD) candidate at Regent University in their Organizational Leadership Program.

She is an award-winning public speaker and has presented in over twenty countries on overcoming adversity, reaching your dreams, computer security, and project management. She served in the Michigan Army National Guard as a communications specialist and was commissioned into the US Army Officer Signal Corps, serving on Active Duty and later the US Army Reserves. She has worked at both the US European Command and the US Northern Command & North American Aerospace Defense Command (NORAD) on multiple communications and IT projects. She served two years as a senior cyber security policy analyst at the Office of Management and Budget, Executive Office of the President and currently works as the Senior cyber security advisor for the Department of Energy Chief Information Security Officer.

Amy's motto is "A woman who is passionate about project management, public speaking, and shoes."

# Learn More at

*amyshamilton.com*

*@ashban (Twitter)*

*@amyshamiltonpmp (Instagram)*

CPSIA information can be obtained
at www.ICGtesting.com
Printed in the USA
LVHW031026080322
712832LV00011B/1374

9 780998 274652